seventeen

real girls, real

D0460281

TRUE
CRIME

real girls, real-life stories

TRUE CRIME

From the Editors of *Seventeen* Magazine

Hearst Books
A Division of Sterling Publishing Co., Inc.
New York

These stories are reprinted from *Seventeen* magazine 2003 to 2007.

Book design by Kelly Roberts

Cover photo: AP Photo/Ric Field

Library of Congress Cataloging-in-Publication Data

Seventeen real girls, real-life stories : true crime / from the editors of
Seventeen magazine.
      p. cm.
   Includes index.
   ISBN-13: 978-1-58816-648-7 (alk. paper)
   ISBN-10: 1-58816-648-1 (alk. paper)
   1. Youth—Crimes against—Case studies. 2. Violence in
adolescence—Case studies. 3. Youth and violence—Case studies. 4.
Juvenile delinquency—Case studies. I. Seventeen
   HV6250.4.Y68S47 2007
   364.1083'5—dc22

                              2006025464

10 9 8 7 6 5 4 3 2 1

Published by Hearst Books
A Division of Sterling Publishing Co., Inc.
387 Park Avenue South, New York, NY 10016

Seventeen and Hearst Books are trademarks of
Hearst Communications, Inc.

www.seventeen.com

For information about custom editions, special sales, premium and
corporate purchases, please contact Sterling Special Sales
Department at 800-805-5489 or specialsales@sterlingpub.com.

Distributed in Canada by Sterling Publishing
^c/o Canadian Manda Group, 165 Dufferin Street
Toronto, Ontario, Canada M6K 3H6

Distributed in Australia by Capricorn Link (Australia) Pty. Ltd.
P.O. Box 704, Windsor, NSW 2756 Australia

Printed in United States

Sterling ISBN 13: 978-1-58816-648-7
         ISBN 10: 1-58816-648-1

contents

foreword

Hey!

This is a collection of the most powerful real-life stories that have ever come across our desks. Some of them have made us cry, others made us angry, many have shocked us beyond belief (and unfortunately, plenty have done all three).

The point of this book isn't to freak you out, but rather to start a conversation so we can all learn from these stories. We learn that life is precious and that every little decision we make can change the course of our lives. And perhaps, most importantly, that no matter how badly we feel or how hard our situation is, there is someone out there who knows exactly where we're coming from.

Just so you're not surprised: Some of these stories are very upsetting. But as you know life isn't always a fairy tale.

—the Editors of *seventeen*

virginity murder

When Jasmine, 12, told her mother that she had lost her virginity, she didn't realize that it would be one of the last things she'd ever say.

A t 5 P.M. on November 26, 2004, the day after Thanksgiving, Chaunetta Robinson, 16, and her mom, Tina, headed out their front door to visit some relatives. As they walked to the car, they heard their 12-year-old neighbor, Jasmine Archie, screaming from inside her house. "It was pretty loud," says Chaunetta. "We stood there listening for a minute, but we didn't think anything of it. Their mom was always yelling—they could have been getting a whipping."

But when they returned four hours later, the street was swarming with police cars. Chaunetta and her mother stood on their porch, watching the commotion. "At a little after 11, they wheeled a stretcher out of the house," says Chaunetta. "It had a white sheet draped over it. Somehow, I just knew it was Jasmine."

UNUSUAL FAMILY

Back in February 2004, Jasmine; her 9-year-old brother, Ja'Corey; and their mother, Tunisia, moved to 1108 Huron Street, in a working-class area of Birmingham, Alabama. Jasmine's father didn't live with them, and her mother didn't make enough money to always pay the bills. Once Ms. Archie even

9

mentioned to her neighbors that all they had to eat was spoiled milk.

But even more than their financial troubles, the Archies were known for their strange behavior. "Jasmine's mom seemed locked in her own world," recalls Ms. Robinson, who's lived in the neighborhood for seven years. When the family first moved in, Chaunetta tried to be friendly to Jasmine, but Ms. Archie made it hard. "She almost never let Jasmine or Ja'Corey go outside, except for school," says Chaunetta. "I felt sorry for Jasmine. The one time I did see her and her brother on the lawn, her mom came out screaming at them to come back in. It was scary. She was acting like a crazy person."

Jasmine didn't have many friends at school either. At about 5 feet 9 inches, she felt self-conscious about towering over the other sixth graders and complained to some of her classmates that boys didn't like her. Still, the girls seemed to. "She was quiet, but she giggled a lot and was nice to everybody," says classmate Tenilya Samuels, 12.

In March, about a month after the Archies moved to town, neighbors spotted Ms. Archie in her backyard sitting in her car—while it was going up in flames— and notified the police. "I didn't know what to think," Chaunetta says. "Was she trying to hurt herself?!" when the cops came, Ms. Archie said that she'd been burning trash in her backyard when the car rolled into it, so she jumped in to get some of her stuff out. But the officers were suspicious enough to ask Cynthia Parham, a social worker, to investigate whether Ms. Archie might be mentally ill.

Later that day, Ms. Parham went to Councill Elementary School, which Jasmine attended, to ask her about her mom. But Jasmine just defended her. "My mom takes care of us," she said. "She cooks and cleans and washes." Ms. Parham had no choice but to believe her.

Still, over the next few months, Ms. Archie's behavior grew more bizarre. In the middle of the sweltering 2004 Alabama summer, neighbors saw her standing in the sun, wrapped in a bulky winter jacket. And that same summer, they saw her sitting in her front yard in a lawn chair—getting soaked during a violent thunderstorm.

SUSPICIOUS BOYFRIEND

Near the end of that summer, neighbors saw a man going to the Archies' house about twice a week. "He drove a nice car," Chaunetta recalls. "It was a new Cadillac, I think. It seemed like he had money." The man was Ms. Archie's boyfriend—who was said to be a married trucker.

But almost as soon as he appeared, ugly rumors began floating around the neighborhood. No one seems to know exactly where or how they began. "People were saying that her mother's boyfriend was having sex with Jasmine," Chaunetta says. "I believed it—he was really creepy and Jasmine looked a lot older than 12. She was developed. I could see why a man might . . . want her."

VIOLENT REACTION

Around 7:30 A.M. on Friday, November 26, 2004, Ms. Archie's boyfriend, who had been coming around for a few months, stopped by with groceries. Right away he and Ms. Archie began fighting, and after a few minutes, he left. Later that afternoon, Jasmine seemed upset about something. "Mom," she timidly said, "I need to talk to you. Can we go for a walk?" Ms. Archie said okay, and the two set off for a nearby park. On their walk, Jasmine told her mother that she'd had sex.

Ms. Archie's lawyer, David Luker, has denied *Seventeen*'s request for an interview with her, and her boyfriend has disappeared, so it's not known if Jasmine told her mom *who* she'd had sex with—whether it was with the boyfriend or not. But either way, Ms. Archie began screaming at Jasmine. When they got back home, the screaming turned into physical fighting. Jasmine ran into her bedroom to try to get away from her mom, but Ms. Archie chased after her. She lunged at her daughter, tackled her, and pinned her to the ground.

"Ja'Corey!" Ms. Archie yelled to her son. "Go in the kitchen and get me the bleach and a cup!" Only 10 years old, the frightened boy did as he was told. He brought the bleach into Jasmine's room and cowered in the corner, as his sister screamed for help. "I want you to watch," Ms. Archie told him. "Don't scream, don't cry, and don't tell anyone. If you do, I'll do the same to you."

Then Ms. Archie, who was sitting on top of her daughter, poured the bleach into the cup, pried open the girl's mouth—and forced it down her throat. Jasmine's body rejected the poison, and she began to vomit. But with her mother still straddling and crushing her, Jasmine couldn't turn over to spit it out. Jasmine struggled, trying to throw her mom off her and gasp for air, but she couldn't do either. For 30 minutes, Ms. Archie stayed on top of her suffocating daughter—until Jasmine stopped breathing altogether.

HORRIFYING CONFESSION

Ms. Archie climbed off her daughter and grabbed Ja'Corey. They didn't have a car or a working phone, so they walked nearly two miles to her mother's house. When they got there at around 7 P.M., she explained that Jasmine wasn't breathing, so Ms. Archie's mother, Bernice, called 911. Then Ms. Archie got into her mother's car and drove back home. She went inside, closed Jasmine's bedroom door, and sat down in the living room to wait for the police to arrive.

Within an hour, the house was swarming with officers. When Detective Warren Cotton, the lead investigator, walked into Jasmine's room, he saw signs of a struggle: Her mattress was half off the bed frame—and Jasmine was lying dead on the floor next to it, with vomit on her clothes. He went back to the living room and sat down with Ms. Archie, who seemed stunned but not upset. "My boyfriend had been in the house earlier," she said to him, almost suggesting that he'd somehow been involved in Jasmine's death.

Three days later, on Monday, November 29, Detective Cotton called Ms. Archie and Ja'Corey into the station for more questioning. He put them in separate rooms, and then went to speak to the young boy first. Ja'Corey looked wide-eyed and frightened, but when Detective Cotton asked him what had happened that night, he knew just what he wanted to say. "My mom was on top of Jasmine," he said with a surprising amount of composure. "She told me to go get the bleach from the kitchen, and when I got back she said I had to watch."

As disturbing as the story was, Detective Cotton believed the little boy: "His version made much more sense, in terms of the evidence we had, than [any] of [Ms. Archie's] stories." With this new information, Detective Cotton strode into the other room and confronted Ms. Archie—who immediately confessed. "I wasn't acting like myself," she said with eerie calm.

13

"I was upset because she'd just told me she wasn't a virgin. I wanted to teach her a lesson, so I told Ja'Corey to get the bleach—and I made her drink it."

LOST SOUL

After confessing, Ms. Archie was arrested and charged with capital murder. On August 22, 2006, she plead *guilty* and was sentenced to life in prison with no parole.

Back on December 4, 2004, one week after Jasmine's death, a small service was held at a nearby church. Her mom didn't leave prison to attend it. "It's so sad," says her neighbor Ms. Robinson, whose heart breaks every time she looks at Jasmine's old house. "Jasmine was secluded in her own little world. Even in the neighborhood, almost no one knew her name." Now, as Jasmine lies in her final resting place—an unmarked grave in Birmingham—she risks being forgotten forever.

fight to the death

Ali, 19, loved chilling out at her summer job at the local pool—until the day a dangerous visitor appeared in the doorway.

A round 5 P.M. on June 18, 2002, 17-year-old Tyler Kemp arrived at the neighborhood pool in Leawood, Kansas, to relieve his sister, Ali, from her shift as an attendant. Ali had asked him to cover for her because she wanted extra time to get ready for a date that night with her boyfriend, Phil. As Tyler pulled into the parking lot, he saw Ali's Jeep Grand Cherokee out front. He parked, walked through the gate, and saw his sister's keys, purse, and cell phone on a table nearby, but he didn't see Ali. Tyler figured she'd run across the street for a snack at Subway. He grabbed the pool skimmer and began cleaning the pool, waiting for her to come back.

Fifteen minutes passed, and Ali still hadn't shown up. This is weird, Tyler thought. He called home and told his mother. His mom told his father, and within minutes Tyler saw his dad, who lived just a few blocks away, enter the gates. "Ali's still not here?" Roger Kemp asked, concerned. He began walking around, looking for clues that would tell him where she might have gone. He walked into the pump house, where he saw the usual clutter of equipment and pool supplies. As he

15

reached the back, Mr. Kemp noticed a large pool tarp crumpled on the floor. He inhaled sharply. There was a leg sticking out from under the tarp.

GOLDEN GIRL

Growing up in Leawood, an affluent Kansas City suburb, Ali had everything going for her. Athletic and outgoing, with brown eyes and chestnut hair that fell to the middle of her back, she'd had the same close-knit group of 10 girlfriends throughout high school. But she was careful not to exclude others. Back in high school she often showed new students around.

"It's hard moving to a place where everyone has grown up together," says Ali's friend Laurel Vine. "So she always brought the new kid to lunch. If she threw a party, she made sure her parents let it be big enough so that nobody was left out." And she was totally in love with Phil, her high school sweetheart.

Ali was looking forward to her sophomore year at Kansas State University, which was going to be busy. Her former soccer coach had asked her to go on a trip to Russia the next year to work with poor children. And a national honor society had picked her as one of sixty students to travel with the US State Department on a learning expedition to France, China, and Australia.

With so much on her plate, Ali appreciated her laid-back summer job at the pool. Even better, she had managed to get Phil and her two brothers jobs there too. The shift was especially easy when the weather was cloudy, because the pool was practically empty except for construction crews who were working nearby. When that happened, Ali would often call her friend Lindsay Courtney. "Can you come over?" she'd ask. "I hate the workmen staring at me. It gives me the creeps."

DEADLY STRUGGLE

Tuesday morning, June 18, had dawned gloomy and overcast. Having been out late the night before with her girlfriends, Ali slept in. Just before 2 P.M., she hopped into her Jeep to head to her shift at the pool. Phil had worked the previous shift and hung around to discuss their plans for that evening: Since Phil was leaving on a family vacation the next day, it was going to be a special dinner for just the two of them. "I love you," he told Ali as he left. "See you later."

According to the suspect's confession to the police — which he later took back — here's what happened: At about 3 p.m., Ali was inside the pump house, where she often went to get supplies to do chores around the pool. A stranger appeared in the doorway. He was big and stocky, dressed in workman's clothes, and carried a bucket of tools. He tried hitting on Ali, but he made her nervous. When Ali asked him to let her out, he blocked the doorway and didn't move. And then he reached out to touch her.

Cornered and frightened, Ali pushed him back, then punched him on the shoulder — and the man exploded in rage. He struck Ali again and again with his fists until she tumbled facedown on the tarp. He landed on top of her, placing his legs on both sides of her body so she couldn't move. She thrashed around, but he began to strangle her. After a few minutes, Ali stopped struggling. The man yanked down her shorts and underwear and tried to rape her, but he couldn't get an erection. So he got dressed, put the tarp over Ali's bruised body, and left.

17

GRISLY DISCOVERY

At about 3:10 P.M., Laurel decided to visit Ali at the pool on her way home from a doctor's appointment. She pulled up at 3:15 P.M., just as a heavyset man in a uniform trudged by. The two glanced at each other indifferently, then the man drove off in his pickup truck. Laurel got out of her car and called around the pool for Ali, but she wasn't there. "I thought she was probably over at the shopping center across the street," Laurel says, "so I went home."

It was two hours later when Mr. Kemp found Ali's body. Throwing back the tarp, he saw Ali lying facedown, naked except for her sports bra and T-shirt, which had been pushed up under her armpits. She was bleeding from the head. "Call 911!" he yelled to Tyler. Kneeling beside Ali, Mr. Kemp took her hand. It was cold. He felt along her forearm—it was also cold. Her back still seemed slightly warm, offering a faint hope that she was alive. Gently he rolled her over. Matted with blood, Ali's long hair obscured her features, and her father gently parted it to look at her. Both of her eyes were swollen; her battered face was dark blue. By the time Mr. Kemp looked up, the paramedics were rushing into the pump room.

"Hold on, honey," he whispered. While the EMTs frantically tried to revive Ali with CCPR, her father repeated softly, "Stay with us, Ali, stay with us, Ali."

She never responded. When the ambulance reached the hospital, Ali was officially pronounced dead.

Laurel had heard about the attack through another friend, and she flew to the hospital, where she quickly tracked down a police officer and told him about the workman she'd seen at the pool. That night Laurel racked her brain to give a detailed description for a computerized portrait of the man she had passed.

SHOCKING CONFESSION

By February 2003, eight months after Ali's murder, the police still couldn't find the workman, their prime suspect. To help, Ali's father had the composite sketch placed on a billboard along with a hotline number — and they got nearly 3,000 leads. Two of the tips pointed to Teddy Hoover, a man who ran a pool-cleaning service. Detectives interviewed him and asked whether he would submit a DNA sample. Hoover replied he would need to consult his attorney. That wasn't an unusual request, detectives say, because most people, even if they are innocent, are nervous about taking a DNA test. But when they reached Hoover's attorney a few weeks later, they learned that their suspect had slipped away. The lawyer told them that Hoover had gone to Las Vegas — but he *didn't* tell them that Teddy Hoover wasn't his client's real name.

"Teddy Hoover" turned out to be Benjamin Appleby, then 29, who had stolen the identity of a dead friend and had served time for robbery and had confessed to exposing himself to young women. Detectives uncovered his real name after a tip led them to his girlfriend in Bantam, Connecticut, a woman who was then living with a man whose last name was Appleby. Finally, in November 2004, Kansas detectives traveled nearly 1,300 miles to Connecticut, where they questioned Appleby about Ali's murder. He broke down.

During his taped confession, Appleby hung his head and rubbed his forearms nervously as he described how Ali had rejected him. "I f***ing lost it," he says. He admitted to strangling her but couldn't remember what he had used to do it. He cried as he described covering her body. "I'm trying to do the right thing," he said, sobbing. "I don't want any sympathy."

But after Appleby was brought back to Kansas to face charges of capital murder and rape, he recanted, saying his confession was made under duress. He's still waiting to go to trial.

PROUD MEMORY

To honor Ali's memory, the Kemps have launched a scholarship fund and TakeDefense.org, a national organization that offers free self-defense classes to women, so that they will know they have the skills to protect themselves—and not just throw a punch in panic, as it seems Ali did. So far it has trained 5,000 women (among them Laurel and Jennifer Wyand, another of Ali's friends). "Ali would have loved all that her father is doing in her name," says Jennifer, "helping to make sure that nothing like this happens to another young girl."

During Appleby's preliminary hearing, a pathologist testified that Ali had violently resisted her attacker, breaking her left index and middle fingers as she struggled. Laurel finds solace in the fact that Ali tried to strike back. "She fought until she couldn't fight anymore. That didn't surprise any of us. Ali loved life too much to give up."

i didn't kill him!

Tawny, 19, knew she didn't cause her brother's death. So why didn't the rest of the world believe her?

A pit opened in my stomach as I pulled onto my street and saw an ambulance, police cars, and a Life Flight helicopter. My dad was yelling, so upset I couldn't make sense of what he was saying. It was total chaos. As I got out of the pickup, three cops approached me. "You killed your brother!" one shouted. Then he grabbed my shirt, spun me around, and cuffed me. I was scared and confused. I had no idea what was going on. I never imagined that my younger brother would be dead at 17—or that I'd be accused of killing him.

BROTHERLY LOVE

Jeff* and I were just two years apart. When I look at old photos and home videos, I see us as babies lying on a blanket together, or as kids practicing karate moves.

My parents divorced when I was 5, and I didn't live with Jeff for several years. Then when he was a sophomore in high school, he came to Utah to live with my dad and me.

I started to see Jeff as a really cool kid with a lot of talent. He had a dry sense of humor, like on *Monty*

Name has been changed.

21

Python. He played guitar and sax, and was on the debate team. He would have made a great politician or lawyer.

SAD DIAGNOSIS

One day when Jeff was 17, he spaced out and didn't respond when I called his name. Minutes later, he snapped out of it. The doctors said he had absence seizures, an epilepsy-like disorder. Another day, he had a grand mal seizure. He fell to the floor shaking and had to be rushed to the ER.

The diagnosis was really hard for Jeff, because his dream was to enter the Air Force Academy; the seizures made that impossible. Worse, his driver's license, which he'd just gotten, was taken away because the disorder made driving risky.

After that, he became really angry. He was constantly doing crazy things, and he even jumped in front of my dad's car once.

TRAGIC FIGHT

On July 8, 2002, I was taking Jeff and my 12-year-old half-brother Mark* on errands. We stopped at the bank, then Jeff wanted to go to Burger King. My dad was making dinner, so I said no. He got really angry and started swearing at me.

I ignored him, and dropped Mark off for a haircut. From the backseat of the pickup, Jeff kept yelling and even threw an ice scraper at me. I said, "I'm taking you home."

When we were about 15 feet from our house, Jeff suddenly pushed the passenger seat forward and reached for the door. All I could get out was, "Jeff, don't . . . wait!" Before I knew it, the door was open and he had jumped out.

22

I hit the brakes and rolled down the window. He was half-sitting, half-lying by the side of the road. I asked if he was OK and he snarled back, "Leave me alone." I decided to let him cool off, thinking he'd walk the few steps home when he was ready. I drove off to pick up Mark. When I got home, the police were waiting for me.

SERIOUS ACCUSATION

I'll never forget the look of terror on Mark's face as we pulled up to that awful scene. We didn't know what had happened. As the officers cuffed me, I learned that Jeff had died--and they thought I'd run him over. At the county jail, I was handed a booking sheet that said "hit and run" and "homicide." I felt so sad and angry at myself for driving off. But I also *knew* that I hadn't hit him.

On my second day in jail, I finally talked to my dad. I told him what had happened; he just cried. I was released after 72 hours since no charges had been filed. When I went to Jeff's funeral the next week, I half expected him, always a joker, to open his eyes and scare us silly. But he didn't.

UNANSWERED QUESTIONS

It took several months for the police to decide whether to file homicide charges. Things with my father were hard during that time. Once, he wondered aloud if I really had hit Jeff. Thankfully, the autopsy found no sign of Jeff having been hit by a car. There was some evidence of head trauma. Maybe he had a seizure while sitting by the curb and fell backward. Or he could have hit his head when he jumped, and that could have triggered a seizure. It's frustrating not knowing exactly how Jeff died, but I'm glad Dad read the report and knew I hadn't killed him. It helped to know I had Dad's support.

I was ultimately charged with failing to remain at the scene of an accident. I pled guilty and received suspended jail time and probation. I was so relieved not to be charged with homicide.

MOVING ON

Often I dream of the afterlife. In good dreams, Jeff is with my grandparents. In my nightmares, he's alone and miserable; sometimes I wake up screaming.

I cope by taking it one day at a time. Soon after Jeff's death, I moved out. I work at a clothing store and go to school for massage therapy. Massage has helped me forgive myself, because I'm learning something I can do to make others feel better.

I also go to a support and counseling group every Thursday morning. One of our recent assignments was to write a letter to somebody we're angry at. I wrote to Jeff—asking why he jumped out of the truck—and to myself too. The anger and guilt won't disappear, but expressing them helps me move forward. That's something I need to do. With all that's happened, I know how short life can be; there's a lot I want to do before my time is up.

school attack

When Edith became a counselor at the
Pleasantville Cottage School, she had no idea
what the girls there had in store for her.

The Pleasantville Cottage School has 16 residential cottages on 175 acres of rolling, green grass in the quiet town of Pleasantville, New York. But this boarding school, for kids 7 and up, isn't always as peaceful as it appears. Most students at the school have been sent there because they've been neglected, abused, or had serious behavioral problems. In fact, the cottages' bedrooms don't have doors, so counselors can easily monitor the school's 200 or so troubled students at all times.

Angenika Carter, one of the Cottage School's residents, was reportedly sent there after being sexually abused and attempting suicide several times. Late one night in August 2001, when Angenika was about 15, she was up at midnight, way past the school's curfew. Edith Toro, the overnight counselor in her cottage, walked into her room. "What's going on?" Edith asked. Angenika glared back at her—she was so sick of adults controlling her. "I'm tired of you!" she suddenly snapped, then she walked over and stuck her face right into Edith's. "I hate you," Angenika hissed.

No student had ever gotten that aggressive with Edith before, and she felt scared. She began to back away, but then Angenika grabbed her and threw her to the ground. Luckily, Edith's cottage co-counselor, Jackie, heard the commotion, came running, and quickly pulled Angenika off Edith. But as the campus security arrived and led Angenika out of the cottage, she punched Edith in the face—as hard as she possibly could.

GOOD INTENTIONS

Edith started working at the Cottage School in 1996, when she was 27. She had a day job in a company's accounts-payable office, but she was putting herself through college and needed extra money. When an acquaintance told her about the school's opening, Edith thought it would be the perfect second job. Because she had grown up in a very poor immigrant family, she thought she'd be able to relate to the kids' hardships. "I hadn't had it easy," Edith says. "I felt I could help." So with little formal training, she began work in Cottage 12, where she spent 11 P.M. to 7 A.M. making sure her 12 teenage girls stayed in bed and didn't sneak out.

Just as she'd thought, Edith really connected with her girls. "They needed love," she says. "And I loved them." If any of the girls in her cottage got sick during the night or couldn't sleep, Edith would let them stay up and read or watch TV with her.

NEW STUDENTS

In 2001, after Edith had been working nights at the school for five years, seven new teenage girls joined Cottage 12. Erica Mateo, Crystal Silva, Takiyah Miller, Lidia Orellana, Nicole Infante, Mary Brown, and Latoya Barcliff were sent to the Cottage School because they'd had difficult lives. When Crystal was 4, her dad pushed her mom out of the window of their sixth-floor apartment—and her mom grabbed onto him as she was falling, killing them both. Lidia was put into foster care when she was just five days old—by the time she was 14, she was reportedly smoking pot and stealing. The girls quickly bonded with Angenika, and as a group, they were more difficult than any Edith had met before.

Since these girls had no one else to lean on, they became like family to one another. Mary would steal her teachers' wallets to get money, and then use it to buy Chinese food as a treat for the others. Latoya helped the other girls do their laundry, Takiyah braided their hair, and Erica helped everyone with their chores. It was nice for them to have each other—but not for Edith. As the girls got closer, they also began helping each other break the rules. They started setting their alarms for the middle of the night and sneaking out together to smoke pot. In fact, they snuck out so much that Edith even started unplugging their alarm clocks so they'd sleep through the night, which drove the girls crazy.

Edith was vigilant, and as the girls began realizing they couldn't get away with what they wanted, they started to get more outspoken. "Stop bothering me!" Takiyah screamed one night around January 2002, as Edith made her rounds. "Go back to China!" The girls agreed that things would be better if Edith were gone.

BRUTAL ASSAULT

On Thursday, February 7, 2002, Edith arrived at work around 11 P.M. About 20 minutes later, she went upstairs to check on the girls. Suddenly Angenika

27

charged out of Mary's room and headed for Edith, her eyes wild with hatred, as if something had snapped inside of her. Scared, Edith turned to race downstairs.

Unlike the last time Angenika had attacked Edith, the cocounselor had left, so Edith had no one to yell to for help. Angenika caught Edith at the bottom the stairs and began to punch her head. The other seven girls gathered around to watch. "Don't hit me!" Edith begged. But that only got the other girls to start yelling, "F*** her up!" Angenika grabbed onto Edith's hair, and she and Nicole dragged her into the living room, while Takiyah began kicking Edith's back. Edith was so confused and scared, she didn't want to fight back. "I though one wrong move might cost me my life," she explains.

The girls continued to beat Edith until Angenika splashed a bottle of rubbing alcohol into Edith's face. "Burn the b****," Latoya said as she handed Angenika a lighter. Angenika flicked it on—and Edith's face went up in flames. It hurt more than she could bear, but still, she thought, I can't die—I haven't even gotten married or had kids yet. Within seconds Edith managed to get to her feet and throw a blanket over her head to put out the flames.

Edith's head was pounding, and her skin was blistering. "Let's go, b****," Angenika said, as she easily shoved Edith down the steps to the basement. The girls raced after her. "We're going to kill you tonight," Angenika said. "Little by little, we're going to make you suffer." Angenika grabbed a fire extinguisher and blasted it into Edith's face. Then Nicole ripped a piece of cable wire from the basement ceiling and wrapped it around Edith's neck. "It would be so easy to kill you," Nicole said, as Erica grabbed a jug of bleach from the nearby laundry room and threw it into Edith's burned face. Edith screamed. "I couldn't take the pain anymore," she says. She finally thought to herself, Just kill me.

As the girls dragged Edith back upstairs to the living room, her skin peeled off her face. "We've got to kill the b****," Nicole said. "Let's just kill the b****." But then a pair of car headlights washed by outside, and Mary shouted, "Some staff is on their way over!" It was 12:30 A.M. By that time, they'd been torturing Edith for more than an hour.

REAL CONSEQUENCES

The girls panicked. Edith, with a final surge of adrenaline, raced out of the back door and headed for the car, which a day counselor from Cottage 14 had just parked. "What happened?!" she asked in horror, as she saw Edith's blistered face and swollen eyes. "They're trying to kill me!" Edith gasped. The counselor immediately called staff supervision, and they raced Edith to nearby Westchester Medical Center and alerted the police.

Meanwhile, the girls fled into the freezing night. Angenika, Latoya, and Takiyah hid inside a boy's cottage, and Nicole and Lidia ran behind the school's gym—but they were all caught and arrested right away. Erica, Crystal, and Mary headed for a nearby bar, where they were able to hitch a ride to Queens, New York, where Erica's boyfriend lived. (Within a five-week search, they were arrested too.)

On February 16, nine days after her attack, Edith was released from the hospital. Her face and chest were still blistered; her arms, legs, and back were covered with bruises and red welts. But three weeks later, determined to go on with her life, Edith went back to her day job. She arrived at work to find that her friends had decorated her desk with flowers and balloons. Edith was so thankful for their support but also relieved that no one asked her what had happened. "I don't like to talk about any of this," Edith explains. "It's too painful."

About eight months later, all eight girls pleaded guilty to assault. In December 2002, before the first sentencing hearings, Edith typed letters to each of the girls, which she planned to present in court. She hadn't had any contact with them since her attack, and she thought confronting them in court might help her make peace with everything that had happened.

On December 17, 10 months after her assault, Edith faced her attackers for the first time as she sat at their hearing. Nervous and sweating, she began to read her letter to Angenika out loud, but tears poured from her eyes, and her voice vanished. James McCarty, the prosecutor, took over: "I hope that you could show some consideration and explain why I became a victim of your rage," he read. When he finished Edith's letter, Angenika said to the judge with a shrug, "I know I was wrong—I don't expect her to forgive me." The judge sentenced all the girls to prison terms, ranging from 1 to 10 years.

PERMANENT DAMAGE

Today, more than two years later, Crystal, now 17, is the only one who is said to have been released. Her social worker says she's trying to move on from this "extremely traumatic time" and won't talk about it.

On the surface, Edith has healed. "Everybody says I look good—but they can't see my scars," she says. There are times Edith still gets so upset that she can't get out of bed, but therapy is helping her understand that the attack was not her fault. "The girls didn't hate *me* so much," Edith explains. "They hated everything. They just got it with me that night because I was the weakest." Edith wishes the girls had reached out for help to deal with their rage instead of lashing out at her. "They didn't have parents to love them, or to tell them what is good and bad," she says. "But just because you don't have a family doesn't mean you can attack somebody We all get angry—there are other ways to handle it."

my nanny molested me

For four years, Lauren, now 21, was horribly abused by a woman who was supposed to take care of her.

M y parents worked a lot when I was growing up in Miami, Florida, so we always had a live-in nanny. In August 1997, when I was 12, my sister, Samantha, was 10, and my brother, Chase, was 5, my parents hired a new nanny named Waldina Flores. "Waldy" was 29 and seemed really cool: She would let me stay up late, and took my side when I fought with my sister. It was great always having her around—she was sort of like a fun second mom.

SHOCKING TURN

One night during my Christmas break that year, Waldy and I were talking in her room. I was chewing gum loudly, so Waldy said, "Lauren stop that smacking." But I didn't. "Fine, I'll do it *for* you," she continued. "Go ahead," I said, laughing. The next thing I knew, Waldy grabbed my head, stuck her lips onto mine, forced her tongue in my mouth—and then pulled out my gum with her tongue! What is she *doing*?! I wondered in shock. I'd never been kissed on the lips before, but it felt like she'd just kissed me. Why would she do that? I turned around and ran to my room. I felt so uncomfortable with what she'd just done. I wondered if I should tell my parents, but it was just so bizarre,

I didn't know *what* I'd say. So instead, I tried to forget about it.

The next day, the first moment we were alone, Waldy turned to me and gently said, "Lauren, I love you, and people who love each other kiss like that." I felt like Waldy *did* love me—like my mom did—so I should believe her. I mean, why would she lie to me?

That night I helped Chase get ready for bed. Most nights Waldy and I curled up with him until he fell asleep, so as Chase drifted off, I wasn't surprised to see her walk in. She lay down behind me—and slowly reached up my nightgown. *What's going on?* I thought, panicking. Then she touched my breasts, and I got even more tense. I didn't want to say anything and freak Chase out, so I just prayed that she'd stop. But then Waldy reached into my underwear and stuck her finger inside my vagina! Now I was *terrified*. I wanted to scream, but I was frozen.

After 15 minutes of Waldy silently touching me like that, she left the room. I lay there, shaking, until I worked up the nerve to confront her. "Why did you do that?!" I asked as I stormed into her room. "It's good for you—you should know what to expect when you have a boyfriend," Waldy calmly explained. *What?!* I thought. But then I hesitated: Maybe she *was* right. I mean, I had never had a boyfriend, and Waldy was an adult with experience, so maybe she *should* teach me about sex. I walked out and didn't tell anyone. I figured now that I knew what to expect from boys, Waldy wouldn't have to show me again.

TERRIFYING CYCLE

The next night, when my parents were still at work and Samantha and Chase were watching TV, Waldy

34

asked me to come into her room. As soon as I did, she came up to me—and started to take off my clothes. "No!" I cried. Waldy picked up her brush and began beating me hard on the back of my neck, screaming, "Don't you love me?!" she was scaring and hurting me, so I said yes, hoping she'd stop. She put the brush down, pushed me on the bed—and began performing oral sex on me. Suddenly my brain shut off, and my body went numb—I wasn't even crying anymore.

After Waldy stopped and left me there, I wanted to tell my parents, but I was too ashamed: Since I hadn't told them as soon as it all started, would they think I'd *wanted* Waldy to touch me? Would they think I was gay? What if Dad got really mad, attacked Waldy, and went to jail? I couldn't risk all that—so I just kept quiet.

DEVASTATING TRUTH

Every day for the next four years, Waldy continued to forced me to have sex—she'd even make me shower in front of her. If I tried to fight back, she'd beat me. I tried to act happy at school and around my parents, so they wouldn't suspect anything. But when I was 16, after four years of abuse, I stopped wanting to eat dinner with my family or to talk to them at all—I guess it got too hard for me to pretend. Mom began worrying and asked me to see a therapist. So I went: If I had an appointment, at least I could be away from Waldy.

Still I was so afraid of Waldy's temper, I told my therapist that I was just under stress at school. But then three weeks later, Waldy came up to me in my room. "Lauren," she said, "when you turn 18, I want to marry you." I was so shocked, I just stared at her. "What, you don't want to?!" she screamed—and then she grabbed my desk chair and threw it at me. That was when I realized I *couldn't* live like this anymore: Waldy wanted to ruin my entire *life*! So I ran out and drove to my therapist's office. "Waldy's been forcing me to have sex with her," I told him. He looked *shocked*. "I'm legally bound to tell your parents," he said. I was still so scared of how they'd react, but I agreed—as long as I didn't have to tell both of them at the same time and deal with their reactions all at once. My therapist called my dad, and he came in. "How did I not see this?" Dad asked, sobbing, as I told him my story.

After the session, my father drove me to a friend's house—and went home to kick Waldy out. She was arrested, charged with sexual battery, and, after pleading guilty, sentenced to 15 years in jail. But I *still* couldn't escape her: Waldy kept writing me letters from jail saying that she loved me.

In May 2004, my dad and I helped pass a law in Florida making it illegal for sexual abusers to contact their victims. It took months of legal work—and almost four years of therapy—to feel free of Waldy. But today, with Waldy in jail and now unable to contact me, I'm no longer living in fear. And I've even learned that I'm able to have a healthy, happy relationship. I'm currently dating a great guy, Kris—and we plan to get engaged soon!

she killed her mom

Nakisha, now 16, was desperate to get away from her mother—but no one imagined she'd take such drastic measure to do it.

O n Friday, May 28, 2004, the school bus dropped off 14-year-old Stephanie Richardson in front of her house in Max Meadows, Virginia. Moments later, her friend Nakisha Waddell, then 14, came racing up the road in her family's blue pickup. Nakisha stopped the truck near Stephanie and stepped out in a frenzy—she was covered in blood. "I did it," Nakisha blurted out. "I killed my mom."

FAMILY TIES

When Nakisha was just a few days old, her father, Tim, left her and her mother, Vaughne. So Nakisha's mom began working three jobs to support her daughter. Then, when Nakisha was 4, her mother married Robert Thomas, a quiet man who worked at a Volvo plant and collected knives. Mr. Thomas's steady job let Mrs. Thomas work less—and spend more time with her daughter. Soon Nakisha and her mom were going to church together almost every week.

"They were so close—more like sisters than anything else," remembers Anna Wilder, Mrs. Thomas's mother, who lived up the road. "We all used to go shopping together, and just sit around, watching TV and laughing." Nakisha was a Girl Scout, and she acted very much like one—she volunteered to help her mom with chores, like grocery shopping, and whenever her grandmother needed something, she'd run right over to help. "Nakisha was also exceptionally intelligent," says Mrs. Wilder. "She loved to read. I used to say, 'Baby, how do you know all those big words?' She'd reply, 'I just know.'"

Nakisha began making lots of friends at church and school. In third grade she met Stephanie Richardson, who lived about a mile away. "Nakisha was quiet," says Stephanie. "And she was nice to everybody." But by the time Nakisha was 13, she was nearly six feet tall and heavy—and her classmates started to make fun of her. Slowly, Nakisha turned self-conscious and moody.

In eighth grade, Nakisha started hanging out with a classmate, Annie Belcher. According to Nakisha's grandmother, Annie introduced Nakisha to drugs like alcohol and pot. As Nakisha spent more time with Annie and her friends, a rift began to form between her and her mom, who disapproved of her daughter's new group. Mrs. Thomas suspected Nakisha was using drugs, but when she tried to talk to her daughter about it, Nakisha closed up. Nakisha also stopped wanting to go to church and started asking to spend time with her biological dad, who Mrs. Thomas thought would be another bad influence. The two started fighting constantly—and Nakisha grew even more distant and secretive. She turned to the Internet and got involved in an online romance with Victor, a sailor in his twenties from Virginia Beach. That was when Nakisha began to fantasize about how great her life could be—if only her mom were gone.

DEADLY THOUGHTS

On the evening of Monday, May 24, 2004, Nakisha told her mom that she wanted to go live with her dad. "Absolutely not," said Mrs. Thomas. "But I hate it here!" Nakisha yelled. "Your father *left* you!" Mrs. Thomas yelled back. "He never paid a penny of child support. Why would he want you *now*?" Nakisha was deeply hurt—she felt like she *had* to get away.

The next afternoon, while Nakisha and Stephanie rode the bus home from school together, Nakisha said matter-of-factly, "I want to kill my mom. Will you help me?" Stephanie just laughed—she assumed Nakisha was joking. "I've heard people say things like that," Stephanie explains. "But they never actually *mean* it."

The following day, Mrs. Thomas came home from work to find Nakisha talking to her dad on the telephone. Mrs. Thomas grabbed the receiver from her daughter and hung it up. "I hate you!" Nakisha screamed. Later she ran into her bedroom and slammed the door.

On Friday, May 28, Mrs. Thomas left for an early shift at the furniture factory where she worked. Mr. Thomas was in Texas visiting his son, so Nakisha was home alone. She called Annie and asked if she wanted to ditch school. Then, at about 8 A.M., Nakisha got into her family's pickup truck—though she didn't have a driver's license—and drove to get Annie.

COLD-BLOODED MURDER

Nakisha spent the morning packing with Annie and figured that after she did what she had to do, she'd go to Virginia Beach to crash with her online boyfriend, Victor, for a while. Around noon, Mrs. Thomas pulled up to the house. She walked inside and jumped when

39

she saw the girls sitting at the kitchen table. "You scared me," said Mrs. Thomas. "Why aren't you in school?" Annie frightened of what was going to happen next, ran into Nakisha's room. "I'm running away," Nakisha said. "And you can't stop me!"

"You're ruining your life!" Mrs. Thomas yelled. "Why are you hanging around with this trash?!" Nakisha screamed back at her mom. "You don't know anything!" Then she picked up a knife that was lying on the kitchen counter—and plunged it into her mother's shoulder.

"What are you doing?!" Mrs. Thomas gasped as she ran out the back door and onto the porch. "You don't know me *or* Dad!" screamed Nakisha, following her mom down the porch steps and into the backyard. "Your dad never wanted you!" Mrs. Thomas yelled, and raised her hands to try to defend herself as Nakisha came at her. But it didn't work: Nakisha began stabbing her mom in the chest, neck, and throat. Blood poured out of Mrs. Thomas, splattering onto the grass and Nakisha—but nothing was going to stop her. Nakisha stabbed her mom 13 times before she fell facedown. Nakisha then knelt next to her bleeding mother and noticed that her chest was still moving—so she methodically stabbed her 30 more times in the back, until she was sure that her mother was dead.

FAILED COVER-UP

Annie came outside and saw Nakisha kneeling beside her mom's body. "Oh, God, Annie," said Nakisha, starting to cry. "What did I do? I don't want to go to jail," she said. "We have to hide the body," Annie replied. "Go get some sheets, and we'll cover her up." Nakisha did what Annie said, but when she got back

40

outside, she lost her nerve. "I can't touch her," said Nakisha, trembling at the gory sight of her dead mother--she couldn't believe what she'd just done.

So Annie took over—she wrapped up Mrs. Thomas's body and told Nakisha to grab her mom's wrists. Then they dragged the body across the lawn to the back shed and covered it with garbage bags. But once they did that, the mound looked messy and totally out of place. "This isn't going to work," said Annie. "We need help." So the girls drove over to Stephanie's house. "We need help getting rid of her," Nakisha pleaded with her friend. But Stephanie was terrified. "You're crazy," she replied. "Get out of here!" Then she ran inside.

Once back home, Nakisha stuffed her bloody clothes and knife into a plastic bag. "We should make it look like a burglary," said Annie. So the girls ran through the house, pulling out drawers and knocking things off tables. Nakisha even went back outside and took the wedding ring off her mother's finger.

By the time the sun came up the next day, the two girls were exhausted—but neither could sleep. They still didn't know what to do with Mrs. Thomas's body—and they were afraid someone would find it. "I think we should burn her," Annie said. So the girls dragged the body out of the shed and about 45 feet into the woods. Nakisha got nail-polish remover and alcohol from the house, and they poured it over her mother. Then they lit matches and set them on the body—but the flame didn't take. "We have to do something," Nakisha said. "My stepdad will be home tomorrow!"

"We should just bury her," Annie finally decided. So the girls went back to the shed for shovels, and after almost four hours of digging in the woods, slid Mrs.

Thomas's body into a shallow grave and covered it with firewood. Finally, around 2 P.M., Annie called her dad and asked if he could pick them up from Nakisha's.

SUDDEN CONFESSION

The next evening, Mr. Thomas arrived home. His house was a complete mess, and his wife was nowhere to be found, so he immediately called the police. Stephanie heard the sirens from down the road and called over to Nakisha's house to see what was going on.

"Who is this?" demanded the man who answered the phone. "I don't know anything," she said, and hung up. But realizing she might get in trouble if she didn't tell them what she knew, Stephanie called back and told the man, a deputy sheriff, what happened—and that Nakisha was probably over at Annie's house.

Within 30 minutes, two officers knocked on the door of Annie's dad's house. Confused, Annie's dad took them back to her room, where the girls were—Nakisha was lying in Annie's bed. The officers stared at the girls. "We know your mom is dead," one of them said. "Where is she?" he asked. Annie was silent. "We buried her in the woods," Nakisha suddenly said in a monotone voice. Then she pulled out a bag of bloody clothes. Immediately, the officers arrested both girls.

LIFELONG CONSEQUENCES

At their hearing, Nakisha plead guilty to murder in the first degree and Annie plead guilty to murder in the second degree. On June 16, 2005, both girls were sentenced. Currently, Nakisha is serving 35 years behind bars and Annie is serving 15 years. They are at a juvenile facility in Christiansburg, Virginia, but will be moved to an adult jail when they turn 18.

Mrs. Wilder, Nakisha's grandmother, recently received a letter, written on pink Hello Kitty stationery, from Nakisha—it was the first contact she'd had with her since the murder. "I know what I did was wrong," she wrote neatly. "But nobody knows what goes on behind closed doors. Sometimes it was so hard to get through the day. I hope you can forgive me, but I understand if you can't," said the letter. "I *hate* what she did," Mrs. Wilder reflects wistfully. "But I still love her--I can't help it."

a tragic night out

Charles, 24, wanted so badly to impress Justina, 19. But in one reckless moment, he cut both of their lives devastatingly short.

Just after 4 P.M. on August 14, 2003, one of the biggest power outages in U.S. history brought the sweltering summer day to a complete standstill. Up and down the Northeast and southern Canada—and as far west as Michigan—computers stopped humming, lights went out, and a noisy world suddenly became eerily silent.

Some New Yorkers would say the dark night that followed was one of the scariest since September 11, 2001. But Charles Kramer, 24, of Staten Island, might have told you it was the most romantic. After all, as thousands took to the sidewalks, hanging out with neighbors they'd never met and wondering when the lights would come back on, Charles first laid eyes on Justina Perugini, 19, the lively, bright-eyed brunette who would consume his attention throughout the fall.

But unlike thousands of others who met during the blackout and vividly remember every weird moment of it, Charles and Justina are no longer here to tell their story—a tragic tale that began on the darkest of nights.

FATEFUL MEETING

Charles, a carpenter who renovated skyscrapers, got out of work as usual that day around 3 P.M. and was

45

one of the lucky ones who beat the blackout home. But there was little to do when he got there—he couldn't watch TV; it was too hot to shoot hoops with his young niece and nephew, as he often did. So as the sun went down, he joined two of his guy friends for a bike ride around Midland Beach, the Staten Island neighborhood where they had all grown up. As they pedaled aimlessly, they got to talking, and Charles, who'd been single for some time, asked his friends if they knew a girl he could meet.

It wasn't that Charles had a problem getting dates. The Derek Jeter look-alike had had several serious girlfriends over the years. Lean, muscular, and tall at 6'1", Charles loved to wear Armani dress shirts and pants, and he took a long time making sure his hair looked just right. But he was also shy and grateful for a setup. His friend Mike, 16, immediately suggested someone he might like: Justina, who lived in nearby Dongan Hills. She was the cousin of his ex-girlfriend Amanda.

Justina was known for her hip, J.Lo-ish style—she lived in cute Nautica sweat suits and big, flashy jewelry. She was easily one of the most fun girls to be around, says her friend Desiree, 20. "She had the long nails, the cigarette in her hand, and the cup of coffee," Desiree remembers. "She was always making a joke or telling you some outrageous story." A tireless storyteller, Justina would hold court on the front steps of her family's two-story home, entertaining her friends with gossip about who was dating whom or cracking them up with wicked one-liners about teachers at school. "She was the show," says her friend Gabriel, 18.

So it was no surprise that on a night with very little else to entertain them, the trio of guys headed to the

Perugini house, where they found Justina and a friend of hers hanging out on the stoop. The group sat on the steps late into the night, chatting and laughing (Justina could do hilarious imitations).

As usual, Charles didn't say much, but he talked about Justina the whole ride home. In many ways, the two were nothing alike: He'd dropped out of school (with his mother's prodding, he eventually got a GED); she was a sophomore at the College of Staten Island and was set on being the first in her family to graduate from college. He was of Puerto Rican descent; she was Italian-American. ("Anything that had to do with Italians, she loved," says her brother Vincent, 29. "*The Godfather, Scarface, Casino* —she liked that genre of movies; she loved the action.") And then, of course, she was one of the most outgoing girls in the neighborhood, and he was reserved around new people. But they did have *some* things in common—one of the most crucial being that, unlike many of their friends, neither drank or did drugs.

UNREQUITED LOVE

Throughout the fall Charles and Justina spoke on the phone and spent a few more evenings on her stoop with their friends. Charles was hesitant about making a move, but "all he did was talk about her," says Mario, 24, one of his closest friends. "He would say over and over, 'Mario, this girl is so *nice*.'"

The problem was, Charles didn't seem to be getting anywhere—until a chilly Saturday in November, when he showed up at her house in a new car. Okay, so he didn't actually *own* the sleek white Nissan 350Z—it belonged to Mario. But he was saving up for one just like it, and when Justina and her cousin asked if it was his, he jumped at the chance to impress them. "Yes," he said winningly. "I just bought it."

His friends now say that Charles had talked about buying that car almost as much as he had talked about Justina. And if you knew him, it made sense that he liked fast cars—Charles had an adventurous side. He'd taught himself to snowboard, played paintball, and rode all-terrain vehicles. Despite his limited income, he and his friends would take off to Florida or the Bahamas, looking for fun. Another thing about Charles—one that his friends still have a hard time believing—is that he had a seriously bad driving record. According to the New York Department of Motor Vehicles, he'd been convicted three times for moving violations, and his license had been suspended six times and was revoked in 1999 for driving without insurance.

The car didn't immediately win Justina over. ("I think he's cute. But he's too shy," Mario recalls her saying later.) But by Monday, there were signs she might be starting to like him back: She talked to her friend Megan about him outside the school cafeteria that morning, and then brought him up again to another friend. "She was saying, 'I'm interested in him. What should I do? Should I go out with him? Should I call him?'" says Vanessa, 20. When Justina got home, she did just that. "She called him and said, 'I'm so happy I met you,'" says Mario, who was hanging out with Charles at the time. And she told her mother she was going out for a drive in a friend's new car.

FINAL RIDE

After dinner with her family, Justina did her hair, put on makeup, and changed into one of her trademark sweat suits. She hung out on the porch talking on the phone as she waited for Charles. "I'm leaving!" she yelled out to her mother as he pulled up.

It was their first date if you ask *his* friends, or a just-friends thing if you ask *hers*. "If she was *really* interested in him, I would have met him," says her mother, Donna. But either way, it was going well at 11:40 P.M., when Justina's friend Gabriel called her to say—as he often did—and asked if she was having fun. She didn't skip a beat. "Yeah," she told him. She was.

No one knows exactly where they were headed, but at 11:46 P.M., they were speeding down Hylan Boulevard, the wide, busy main drag. Charles may have been pumped up about being out alone with Justina, or he may have been trying to show her how fast the car could go. He might even have been racing another driver (there were two other 350Zs on the road as well, according to the police). Only one thing is for sure: As he approached a red light at the intersection of Lincoln Avenue, he floored it, blasting though at 90 miles an hour just as it turned green.

Of course, the perfect timing of a near-miss like this one *could* impress a girl if it didn't terrify her. But Charles wouldn't even have had a chance to catch Justina's reaction. Just past the intersection, he hit a dip and, because he was driving so fast, he lost all control of the car.

The chassis slammed into the dip with a deafening crash. Sparks flew as the car spun out and went careening across two lanes. After spinning around until it was facing the traffic it had just passed, it crashed into a telephone pole. The force sent bumpers, seats, and pieces of carpet flying through the air, landing as far as 100 feet away. And it twisted the car so tightly around the pole that the front and rear tires were actually touching.

Justina died on impact—the passenger compartment was smashed so badly that it was all but obliterated. Charles was still alive, pinned inside the car. A rescue team worked for more than 20 minutes prying his legs from the twisted steel and then rushed him to the hospital. He had broken his cervical spine and split his diaphragm and right kidney. He died four hours later.

BITTER FEELINGS

Now, after five months, friends and families are still trying to cope with the pain. Vincent has instinctively picked up the phone countless times to call his sister since the accident, but he's never once picked up the phone to call Charles's family. He's still too angry. "She was 19, and everything was falling into place for the kid," he says. "And then somebody came along and ended her future. Stopped it right there." But the fact is that *two* promising young people died that night. "We all make bad judgments, but we don't die from them," says Charles's sister, Laurie, 32 "Unfortunately he *did*—and she died with him."

miscarriage or murder?

Nakita, 19, got pregnant when she was just 13.
Now her baby is dead—and she blames her mom.
Here's her side of the story.

O n Wednesday night, March 14, 2001, 13-year-old Nakita Smith leaned back on her living-room couch and screamed in pain. Her mom, Julie Smith, a nurse in Marshall, Arkansas, sat at Nakita's feet, waiting to deliver her daughter's premature baby. Nakita's contractions made her feel like her insides were being ripped open, and she began to sob. But 15 minutes later, at about 11:30 P.M., Nakita gave birth to a baby boy.

MOTHER AND DAUGHTER

Julie Smith had moved to Marshall with her children, Nakita and Joel, then 2 and 7, respectively, in 1989, after she and their dad, Larry, divorced. Marshall is a small town, and life there was hard for Smith—she barely made enough money to take care of her kids. Every few months their electricity would get turned off because she couldn't pay the bill—and there were lots of times when all she could afford to feed them for dinner was a can of soup that had to be heated on their wood-burning stove.

But what kept the Smiths happy was the fact that they had each other. Nakita and her mom had fun just dancing around the house together. "When I was little, I'd visit my dad during the summer," Nakita says, "But I'd have to come back early because I'd miss my mom."

In 1995, Joel started not getting along with Smith, so he went to live with his dad in Texas. Nakita says that's when her mom started to get paranoid that she and 8-year-old Nakita would grow apart. Smith couldn't bear the thought that Nakita might eventually leave too, so she slowly started to let Nakita do whatever she wanted. All that mattered to Smith was that Nakita was happy living with her. Nakita says that by the time she was 13, her mom let her skip school—she missed more than 30 days in seventh grade—and go out with any guy she wanted.

DANGEROUS LOVE

On August 14, 2000, Nakita, 13, was outside a friend's house when she saw a muscular guy drive by in a pickup. "He was so good-looking!" she says, "So I waved. He almost got into a wreck turning around to meet me."

That night Nakita and David,* who was 20, spent hours talking—and they immediately became a couple. After just a week, they had sex for the first time.

Since David didn't want to use a condom, Nakita didn't pressure him to, but they talked about what would happen if Nakita got pregnant. "I'll stay with you—I'll take care of the baby and take care of you," he promised her. Since Nakita was in love, she believed him.

The more time Nakita spent with David, the less time she spent in school. On September 13, a month after they met, school officials asked social workers to begin monitoring Nakita's attendance and behavior.

*Name has been changed.

SCARED SICK

A few weeks later, Nakita started eating more than she ever had—ice cream, cookies, pickles—and acting moody. One day, she says, her mom just asked, "Are you pregnant?!" Even though Nakita feared it might be true, she didn't want to believe it, so she said, "No!" But then, a few mornings later, Smith woke up her daughter, handed her a pregnancy test, and told her to go into the bathroom. After several minutes Nakita walked back into the kitchen, where her mother was nervously waiting, and handed her the plastic stick. Smith placed it on the counter, and a pink line gradually appeared—Nakita was pregnant.

"Oh, s**!" Smith yelled, as a terrified Nakita backed away. Nakita then saw her mom kick their stove so hard that it fell over. According to Nakita, her mom was getting even more worried that she'd lose her. She was afraid that if Nakita's social workers found out she was pregnant, they'd put her into foster care. "We're going to find some way of dealing with this," Smith told her. Then, Nakita says, over the next few days, her mom began pressing hard on her belly, hoping it would make her miscarry. She also started giving her chamomile tea with black pepper, which she'd heard ended pregnancies.

But as Smith was seemingly trying anything to make her daughter lose her baby "naturally," Nakita began resenting her mom and wanting to *keep* her baby. She started pretending to drink her mom's tea mixture—but secretly poured it out. She also began staring in the mirror, imagining herself holding a baby. "It started to make me feel good that I was going to be a mom," she says. But since *her* mom didn't want her to have the baby—and David didn't even believe that she was really pregnant—she was afraid to speak up.

53

DESPERATE ACT

By January 2001, when Nakita was four months pregnant, Smith made her start wearing baggy blouses to hide her growing belly. At this time, Nakita says that her mom thought it was too late to induce a miscarriage, so she'd stopped making the tea. Instead Smith talked about moving to Hot Springs, Arkansas, right after the baby was born—and telling everyone that it was hers.

But then on March 1, when Nakita was about six months pregnant, one of her social workers asked her if she was pregnant. Nakita said no and rushed home to tell her mom. At that point, Nakita says, Smith decided that Nakita needed to have her baby right away—even though she still had three months to go in her pregnancy. That way, she'd no longer be pregnant on March 14, when she had to appear in court for her truancy. Nakita says her mom was scared that if she went there pregnant, the court officials would notice her belly—and take Nakita away.

So on March 12, Smith put on a rubber glove, walked Nakita into the bathroom, and made her sit on the toilet. Then, Nakita says, her mom stuck a scalpel inside her to break her water, so she would deliver the baby. Nakita felt some pressure and then liquid rushed out of her. She didn't feel any pain. "I thought I was ready to go into labor and just needed help along," Nakita explains.

But Nakita didn't go into labor that night. Though she'd started having light contractions the next day, it wasn't until two nights later, while Nakita and her mom were driving back from her court date (where they'd successfully hidden her pregnancy), that Nakita's contractions began to get strong. During a very painful one, she squeezed the car door handle so hard that she broke it off.

As soon as they got home, Smith told Nakita to lie down and spread her legs so she could see if Nakita was ready to deliver. The contractions were coming faster, but they decided not to call and tell David, as he'd recently broken up with Nakita. "Hold on!" Smith told her daughter. Nakita screamed in pain. Just 15 minutes later, Smith declared, "It's a boy!" Nakita saw that his blood-covered body fit into her mom's hand — his frail legs hung about two inches down her arm. She says that he opened his eyes and took a breath, but his chest looked sunken. Nakita named her baby Joseph-- and fell asleep.

UNEARTHED SECRET

Smith rocked Joseph for about two hours--until he stopped breathing.

At 6:30 A.M., she nudged Nakita awake to tell her that he'd died earlier that morning. Very hazy from blood loss, Nakita fell back asleep. Smith put Joseph's body in a cotton-ball bag and buried him out back.

Over the next year, Nakita occasionally visited her baby's grave to put wildflowers on it — even though her mom insisted that she continue to keep him a secret. But then on March 11, 2002, almost a year after Joseph's death, Nakita crawled into her closet—and cut her wrists with a knife. "I started thinking about him and . . . wished he was around. . . . ," she trails off. She'd decided that since Joseph had died, she wanted to die too.

An hour later Smith found Nakita crying. "Are you okay?" she frantically asked her bleeding daughter. But Nakita pushed her away. A family friend came to take

Nakita to a counseling center, where she finally broke down and admitted everything. Though she knew her mom would be mad, she says it was a relief: "I finally didn't have to keep it to myself."

ONGOING SAGA

Eleven days later investigators arrested Nakita's mother for first-degree murder. Then, on April 21, 2004, at age 17, Nakita testified against her mom in court, tearfully telling her story. But Smith (who declined *Seventeen*'s request for an interview) testified that she only broke her daughter's water because Nakita was already in labor—she said that the whole thing was just a tragic miscarriage. Ralph Blagg, Smith's lawyer, claimed that the baby had just been too small to survive. Though some of the jurors hearing the case thought Smith was guilty of a crime, they couldn't come to a unanimous decision, so a verdict wasn't reached and the judge declared a mistrial. Nakita sobbed for her dead baby. Smith was retried, with the charge reduced to manslaughter. She plead guilty and was sentenced to 72 months probation and received fines.

In the meantime, Nakita lives with her dad in Madisonville, Texas, where she has stayed for the past few years. She's still trying to come to terms with everything that's happened. "I know I made a mistake by having sex that early," she pauses, thinking about how much she loves her baby, "but I'll never see Joseph as a mistake."

lesbian killers

Holly, now 17, was furious that her grandparents forbade her to see her girlfriend— so she decided to make them pay.

Holly Harvey, 15, had been living with her grandparents Carl and Sarah Collier for about four months while her mom, Carla Harvey, was in prison on drug charges. Things had *not* been going well. On Monday, August 2, 2004, at about 5 P.M., Holly lit a joint in her bedroom in the Colliers' Fayette County, Georgia, basement—just to tick them off. The ploy worked: After a few minutes, Holly heard their footsteps pounding down the stairs.

"I can't believe you're doing drugs down here!" Mrs. Collier, 73, yelled as she marched into Holly's room. "Do you want to end up like your mother?" Holly just rolled her eyes and said nothing. Meanwhile, Mr. Collier, 74, walked to the closet to grab a suitcase for a trip. As his wife turned to follow him, Holly pulled an eight-inch kitchen knife from her jeans, closed her eyes, and plunged it into Mrs. Collier's back. The older woman screamed, but before she could turn around, Holly had stabbed her two more times. At that point Mr. Collier tried to grab the knife from Holly, and they struggled for the weapon. Holly won— and 10 minutes later Mr. and Mrs. Collier were both dead.

ROUGH CHILDHOOD

Growing up, Holly had moved around a lot because her mother was in and out of jail for DUI and drugs. Whenever her mom was arrested, Holly would stay in or around Fayetteville, Georgia, with her uncle, her grandparents, or her mom's friends.

In spring 2002, Ms. Harvey was in jail once again, and Holly, then 13, went to stay with her uncle, Kevin Collier. At first the two got along well, and Holly did what she was told — including chores, like cleaning the bathroom. But once her mom got out of jail and moved in with them, Holly felt she didn't have to listen to her uncle anymore, so she started refusing to do anything he asked. Eventually Holly's rebelliousness escalated to the point where she was caught shoplifting cosmetics at Wal-Mart (and had to pay the store back). Then she was suspended from school for having a bottle of prescription drugs that didn't belong to her.

FORBIDDEN LOVE

Holly started seventh grade that fall, and in middle school she met Sandy Ketchum. The two girls had a lot in common: Both were tomboys who liked to write poetry and listen to hard-core rap. Both experienced troubled upbringings. (Sandy's mom had abandoned her when she was a baby, and she'd been raised by her father and three different women over the years.) And they were also into drinking alcohol and smoking pot — but Sandy also experimented with harder drugs too, like crack and mushrooms. Holly and Sandy became inseparable, and Holly even cut her hair short like Sandy's.

In April 2003, Ms. Harvey was arrested yet again, and Holly went to live with family friends. A year later she moved in with her grandparents, who were hoping they could help Holly turn her life around. They had strict rules: no smoking in the house, no drinking, no drugs. They wanted to know where Holly was at all times—and who she was with. When Mrs. Collier met Sandy, she was instantly suspicious of the girl in the bandanna, oversize shirt, and baggy pants. She asked around and learned that Sandy had been arrested a few times for running away. Mrs. Collier told Holly that she couldn't hang around Sandy anymore. "We're in love!" Holly retorted. Mrs. Collier was shocked. "Two women together is an abomination!" she yelled. Holly wrote a poem about her anger—the last line read, "*All I want to do is kill.*"

By July 2004, Holly had had enough of sticking to her grandparents' rules. She packed a bag, sneaked out of the house, and went to Sandy's mother's home. The girls stayed up late watching TV and smoking pot. When Holly didn't come home, Mrs. Collier called the police to report her as a runaway. The cops tracked her down and brought her home two days later. The next week Holly and her grandparents had to appear in court, and Holly was put on probation for a year. As they left the courthouse, Holly angrily told her grandfather, "I'm going to kill you for making me do this."

DEADLY PLAN

On Sunday, August 1, Holly secretly brought Sandy into her grandparents' basement. That night the two stayed up smoking pot and crack. They were so wired that they couldn't sleep, so Sandy suggested they take Holly's grandparents' Chevy truck to get something to calm them down. "We'll have to kill them to do that," said Holly, who for the past few days had been thinking about doing just that. Suddenly she came up with a plan. She grabbed a pen and wrote the words kill, keys, money, jewelry on her arm. Then she hurried upstairs and pulled three large knives from a wooden block on the kitchen counter. "We have to practice first," she told Sandy when she returned to her room. Holly raised a knife and stabbed her bed. "Like this. Try it." They practiced for several minutes on the mattress.

At around 5 P.M., Holly and Sandy hid the knives and Holly lit the joint to lure her grandparents downstairs. "Quick, hide under the bed," Holly told Sandy when she heard their footsteps. After Holly had stabbed Mrs. Collier and struggled with both adults for the knife, her grandparents caught hold of her arms and pinned her to the bed. "Why aren't you helping me?" Holly shouted to Sandy, who was still hiding. At that moment Sandy jumped out with a knife in her hand and stabbed Mrs. Collier in the chest. Terrified, Mr. Collier turned and ran upstairs. "Go get him! He's gonna call 911!" Sandy yelled. Holly chased her grandfather into the kitchen. When she caught up, he had the phone in his hand, so Holly ripped the cord from the wall. Holly was too fast and too strong for him—she took her knife and stabbed Mr. Collier in the neck. Blood spurted all over her, but she kept stabbing until he fell dead on the linoleum floor in a puddle of blood. Meanwhile in the basement, Sandy stabbed Mrs. Collier over and over. Finally the older woman stopped fighting back.

TWO FUGITIVES

Once both of the Colliers lay dead, Holly and Sandy knew they had to get out of the house. Holly grabbed a duffel bag, threw the knives inside, then drove off in her grandparents' Chevy with Sandy. The girls were covered in blood, so they decided to go to the house of Sandy's friend Cara Polk, 16, to take a shower. "What happened?" Cora asked them at the door. "We killed my grandparents," said Holly, smiling. Stunned, Sara offered them a towel but told them they couldn't come in. Holly and Sandy wiped off the blood and changed clothes in the driveway. After they left, Sara told her parents what had happened and called 911.

Around midnight Holly and Sandy arrived at Tybee Island, a small beach community near Savannah. They had no money, food, or place to stay. As they were near the beach they met Brian Clayton, 22, and his younger brother. Holly told them she and Sandy had run away from home and needed a place to crash, and Brian took them to his house. The next afternoon Holly and Sandy heard helicopters overhead. Sandy went to the window and saw police officers swarming the house. Within minutes the police were inside. "I'm so sorry," Sandy cried as several cops handcuffed her. "Those people didn't deserve to die." But Holly started giggling. "Are they all the way dead?" she later asked.

Sandy confessed and cooperated with the police. On April 14, 2005, both girls pleaded guilty in court to two counts of murder. When the judge asked Holly why she had stabbed her grandparents, she said, "For Sandy. So that we could be together." Both Holly (whom a sheriff described as "cold-blooded" and "cocky") and Sandy were sentenced to life in prison. They are currently serving their terms at separate Georgia prisons.

Today, Kevin Collier still struggles to make sense of his parents' brutal murders, and plans to sell their house and move to another town. "My parents were always there for Holly," he says. "It's hard to believe she did that to two people who loved her."

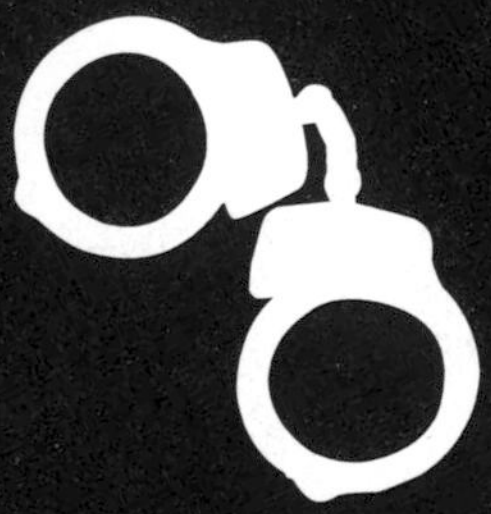

an imperfect crime

In a desperate bid to save their family home, these 14-year-old twin sisters did the unthinkable: They robbed a bank.

On the morning of October 29, 2002, two young girls burst into the Barnegat, New Jersey, branch of the Sun National Bank. One of them held what looked like a silver handgun. "Give me your money," she demanded of the teller. "What is this, a joke?" asked the teller, since it was Halloween week and the girls seemed too young to be actual robbers. "No, I'm not f***ing playing," answered the girl, her face obscured by a black knit ski mask. "Give us your money." Her sister, wearing a black nylon skull cap pulled so tightly it was almost transparent, held out a trash bag to be filled with cash. The teller gave up what she had: $3,550. Then the two girls ran outside and jumped into their getaway car, a 1992 Buick Skylark. Their mother was waiting behind the wheel.

PLANNING THE HEIST

Fourteen-year-old twin sisters Chelsea and Elysia Wortman thought their family was in serious financial trouble. The girls' stepfather, Kevin Jones, a six foot four, 310-pound construction worker (and convicted cocaine dealer) had been recently hospitalized for congestive heart failure and was unable to go back to work. The girls' parents, who had been having financial troubles for years, had filed for bankruptcy protection to save the house from foreclosure. At the time of the robbery, up to 12 people lived in the four-bedroom house: Chelsea and Elysia; their mother and stepfather, Kathleen and Kevin Jones; their sister, brother, and two stepsisters; Kevin's mother and brother; a friend; and a former coworker.

The morning of the heist the girls overheard two troubling phone calls: one from a lawyer saying bankruptcy proceedings were stalled, which meant they could still lose their home; the other about an overdue phone bill, says Supervising Assistant Ocean County Prosecutor Michel Paulhus, who later prosecuted Kevin Jones. "We were having money problems in our house and my family was upset," Chelsea testified later. So she quickly thought of a plan: "I decided to rob a bank."

When she told her mother about her plan, Kathleen Wortman Jones, 34, laughed and resisted. "She told me, 'You are *not* doing this. You're going to get into trouble,'" Chelsea recalled. But Chelsea insisted, "No, I'm for real. We need this money," and began to prepare by painting the orange tip of her brother's plastic BB gun with metallic nail polish to make it look more dangerous.

Within an hour, Kathleen had agreed to a plan to rob a bank that was just five minutes away. Initially Kathleen, Chelsea, and Chelsea's stepsister Devinee, then 16, were in it together. But on their ride to the bank, Devinee decided the plan was too risky, so they

virginity murder

see page 9 for story

mother held in daughter's death

pouring bleach down her throat, police say

...pouring bleach down her daughter's throat and sitting on her until she suffocated, court records sh...

...rimmed and the front wind...

she asked a judge to appoint a lawyer, b... did not ask to attend Jasmine's funeral

"It's unspeakable," Birming... cide Sgt. Scott Pray...
w...

After she was killed by her mother, Jasmine was buried in this unmarked grave in Birmingham, Alabama.

THE DAUGHTER

THE MOTHER

BLEACH

THE WEAPON

see page 15 for story

fight to the death

THE ACCUSED

Appleby is awaiting trail. He confessed to the crime, then later changed his story.

Ali, was about to enter her sophomore year at Kansas State University when she was brutally killed.

THE VICTIM

school attack

see page 25 for story

GUILTY
sentence to 2½ years
Latoya, 15

GUILTY
sentence to 1-3 years
Mary, 15

GUILTY
sentence to 3½-10 years
Angenika, 15

GUILTY
sentence to 2½-7½ years
Nicole, 15

GUILTY
sentence to 5 years
Takiyah, 16

GUILTY
sentence to 1½-4 years
Lidia, 16

GUILTY
sentence to 1-3 years
Crystal, 14

A group of girls at the Pleasantville Cottage School in Pleasantville, NY, had no one to lean on, so they became like family to one another. As the girls got closer, they also began helping each other break the rules.

THE VICTIM

Edith at her home. She doesn't want people to ask about the attack so she won't show her face.

The stairs Angenika threw Edith down.

see page 33 for story

my nanny molested me

Ex-nanny sentenced in sex abuse cas

THE NANNY

THE VICTIM

Flores used to go on vacations with Lauren's family. Now they've cut her out of their photos.

she killed her mom

see page 37 for story

THE MURDERER

Nakisha from Max Meadows, Virginia, was a freshman in high school when she stabbed her mother, Vaughne Thomas, 43 times.

THE MOM

Vaughne Thomas, holding her baby daughter Nakisha.

Nakisha used a hunting knife like this one.

THE WEAPON

Nakisha chased her mom off the porch. After the murder, she and Annie dragged Mrs. Thomas's body to the shed.

see page 45 for story

a tragic night out

At 90 mph, this Nissan hit a dip in the road and slammed into a pole. The car was so crushed that the front and rear tires actually touched.

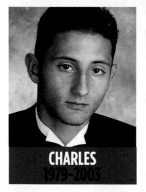

CHARLES
1979-2003

JUSTINA
1984-2003

Donna, Justina's mom, remembers her daughter.

miscarriage or murder?

see page 51 for story

THE DAUGHTER

Nakita in April 2004, during the trial in which she had to testify against her mom.

Hung jury produces a mistrial for nurse in grandson's death

THE MOM

Arkansas Democrat-Gazette/STEPHEN B. THORNTON

First-degree murder defendant Julie Smith enters the Searcy County Courthouse in Marshall after a lunch break during her trial Friday afternoon.

Joseph's burial bag

ARKANSAS STATE POLICE
L·OO·KΩ·O L
"SAY NO TO DRUGS"

Smith was ultimately sentenced to 72 months probabtion.

see page 63 for story

an imperfect crime

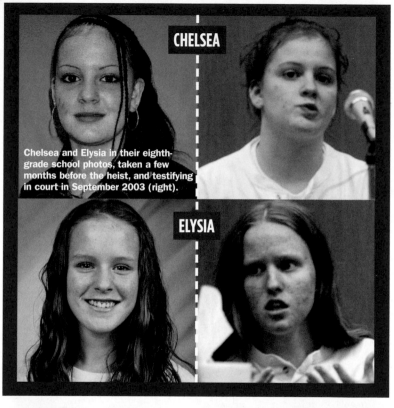

CHELSEA

Chelsea and Elysia in their eighth-grade school photos, taken a few months before the heist, and testifying in court in September 2003 (right).

ELYSIA

The house Elysia and Chelsea tried to save. Right, their mother, Kathleen, and their stepfather, Kevin.

MOM & STEPDAD

the woman who seduced teenage boys

see page 71 for story

Johnson (left) apologized to the boys at her sentencing.

Johnson's house, where she had sex with teenage boys. Right, Johnson and one of her victims.

THE MOM

A VICTIM

See page 79 for story

dying to get high

MELLIE

MARIA

Mellie and Maria (right) met at St. Vincent Ferrer High School, where they quickly bonded over their love of punk rock.

CO-EDS DOOMED BY THE 'HIGH' LIFE

Mellie died in a ninth floor apartment at 84 East Houston Street in New York City.

Maria's younger sister, Karla, and her parents, Marci and Juan Carlos Pesantez, in mourning at Maria's burial.

girl still missing

see page 85 for story

Fred Murray printed "missing" flyers. They were posted as far away as Florida.

MISSING

CALL
(603) 787-2222

MISSING
02.09.04
Maura Murray
Age 21

height - 5'7" weight: 120lbs.
curly brown shoulder length hair

Last seen wearing pants & dark coat

Contact Haverhill P[...]
603-787-22[...]

On February 9, 2004 year Maura crashed her car while driving along Route 112.

MAURA

Maura with her boyfriend, Bill, in 2003.

see page 91 for story

natural born killers

Tony, 19, killed so he could keep dating 13-year-old Tiffany. She helped him cover his deadly tracks.

THE MURDERER

THE GIRLFRIEND

Tony (right) with his father, Anthony. Tony stabbed his father to death on June 25, 2004.

ON THE ROAD TO CAPTURE

WA
WERE CAUGHT HERE
MT
THEY STARTED HERE
CA
HI
NEVER MADE IT HERE
FL

Chargualaf's apartment in University Place, Washington, where his son, Tony, murdered him.

josh's suicide

see page 99 for story

If, I dont wake up tomorrow, I want everyone to Know that I love them.
I did what I did because I was weak, I couldnt handle life, it was to hard.
I will be the first to admit that I am weak I tried to be strong, a lot of people got hurt because I wanted to feel strong, but Im not. I want everybody to know especially Cynthia and Jared and our baby that I tried to live life on lifes terms, but life asked to much of me. Nobody did anything wrong, I just feel so alone in myself, that I cant handle it anymore. I love you all.
Cynthia, I love you so much baby. Please take care of our child and please never forget me.
Tony, Im sorry I had to go but tell the kids that I love them Jamie Give the boys kisses and hugs for me.
Josh the boys dont know me but please tell them about me.
Sara. I love you, please be strong

At my, funeral please play the song. "If I can be like that" by 3 doors down.
Im sorry for my wrongs. Please forgive.

JOSH

Tell Cynthia and Jared that I love them

When Josh hung himself on June 13, 2004, he left this letter behind.

JOSH
1983-2004

Friends and family go here to pay their respects.

HORNE

see page 105 for story

angel of death

"ANGEL OF DEATH"

THE KILLER

Somerset Medical Center

four hours later.   cancer Sept. 5.

'Now I know what happened'

Wide cross-section of survivors comes to see justice done

THE DAD

Christopher Brian Hardgrove
November 8, 1964
August 11, 2003

Twenty Third Psalm
The Lord is my shepherd, I shall not want. He maketh me lie down in green pastures; He leadeth me beside the still waters. He restores my soul, he leadeth me in the paths of righteousness for his name's sake. Yea, though I walk through the valley of the shadow of death, I will fear no evil; for Thou art with me, thy rod and thy staff they comfort me. Thou preparest a table before me in the presence of mine enemies; thou anointest my head with oil; my cup runneth over. Surely goodness and mercy shall follow me all the days of my life; and I will dwell in the house of the Lord forever.

Sheenan Funeral Home
233 Dunellen Avenue
Dunellen, New Jersey 08812

CULLEN PLEADS

killed for being pregnant

see page 111 for story

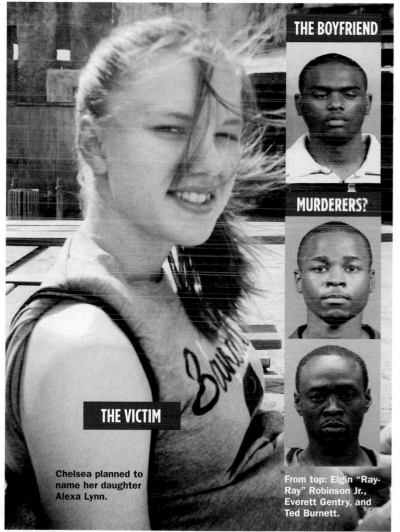

THE BOYFRIEND

MURDERERS?

THE VICTIM

Chelsea planned to name her daughter Alexa Lynn.

From top: Elgin "Ray-Ray" Robinson Jr., Everett Gentry, and Ted Burnett.

see page 117 for story

a mom who loved too much

PS 146 911

Mary McGuire Beam (center), and her 13-year-old daughter, Yamile (bottom right).

dropped her off back home. It was then, Paulhus says, that Kathleen ordered Devinee to "go get Elysia."

A few weeks before, the family had started going to church again, so right before the heist, Chelsea and Elysia paused, dropped to their knees, bowed their heads, and prayed. Then they burst through the bank doors.

A DONE DEAL

After they pulled off the heist, the twins and their mother went back home, passing a cop car speeding toward the bank. They walked in, Kathleen slapped the money on the kitchen table, and Chelsea announced, "We did it." Their stepfather flipped out. "I was raging, telling them to get the f*** out of my house," testified Jones, 38. But instead he ended up driving his wife, the twins, and Devinee to Atlantic City that afternoon. Jones did this, he says, because he panicked and wanted to get away from town. However, prosecutors allege that the adults laundered the stolen money by gambling at Caesar's casino—the idea was to cash in their chips for different dollar bills so the money wouldn't be traced to them. Meanwhile, the girls shopped at a nearby mall.

ON THE TRAIL

By the next night, the family was back from Atlantic City and the Barnegat police were starting to put the pieces together. They saw the twins get out of a car at a convenience store, and made the connection between them and the petite figures in the grainy surveillance photos caught by the bank cameras. The police were able to get the license plate number of the car, which was registered to Jones. On November 1, three days after the robbery, a SWAT team raided the Joneses' home to apprehend the people they believed had robbed the bank at gunpoint. The officers brought the twins and their mother, whom they suspected was involved, down to the police station.

Kevin Jones wasn't home at the time, but his mother was. She proclaimed her stepgranddaughters' innocence as they were being led away. But Detective Sergeant Michael Duffy, who was present when the girls were arrested, says Elysia blew their cover right then and there. "Grandma, shut up. Me and Chelsea robbed the f***ing bank," Duffy heard her shout.

COMPLICATED GIRLS

"When we picked them up, the twins had a tough shell around them," the detective sergeant remembers. "But after we started talking to them, they softened up and were very respectful, very polite." At first, Chelsea tried to take responsibility for the crime, which, according to friends and family, was typical of her. They describe her as a "mother hen" who likes to take charge and fix problems. "She is the caretaker," says stepsister Danelle, 16. "She wants to help everybody." But she's also loud and outspoken and often clashed with her teachers. She likes Jay-Z and Ja Rule and dresses like the rap stars she idolizes—covering her head with bandannas or wearing her long, dark hair in cornrows.

Elysia, a blue-eyed strawberry blonde, is more introverted than her sister. She's a huge Mariah Carey fan, loves singing along to her ballads, and enjoys sketching and cooking. But like her sister, Elysia has a tough side. After a string of fights at school and frequent absences, the school administration ordered her to be tutored at home. "I don't think Elysia had the maturity to weigh what was right and what was wrong," says friend Tiffany Ford, 17, who has known the girls since 1997 and lives two blocks away. "I don't think she understood what would happen if they got caught. But Chelsea—she knew what would happen. She was down for the ride, would do whatever."

In the interrogation room at the Barnegat police station, the questioning dragged on all night. By morning, Duffy had patiently secured confessions from the twins and their mother. As the girls were led away in handcuffs to a youth shelter, they asked to see Duffy once more. He met them outside the police station and, though the girls were handcuffed, they both grabbed his jacket. It was the closest they could come to giving him a hug.

GOOD TIMES, BAD TIMES

The twins never really knew their biological father. Kathleen Wortman left him when the girls were very young, and a few years after the divorce, their father completely vanished. Eventually Kathleen met Jones, and the couple had a daughter, Kiannah, now 11. As pretcens, the twins attended Mt. Zion Baptist Church in Barnegat with their family, where the girls sang in the choir and were known as cheerful and obedient. "They were model children," says their pastor, Reverend Richard Bell.

Their friend Tiffany recalls that when she first met the family, they had an orderly home. "It seemed like they had money, a nice car, a nice living room set," she says. "You had to take your shoes off in the house, couldn't put your hands on the glass table, or talk with your mouth full."

This orderly life apparently started to change as Chelsea and Elysia approached their teens. Money tensions mounted, and Kevin and Kathleen started fighting. And the girls were rebelling. They began smoking and, says Jones, "they didn't want to go to school," partly, he explains, because they felt out of place. Chelsea and Elysia's mother is white and their stepfather is black—and Barnegat is a predominantly white town.

The school situation only got worse in middle school, when both girls came down with mononucleosis and missed three months of classes. When they got better, Jones says they had zero interest in going back to school. That's when Elysia was transferred to the home-tutoring program. "She couldn't function in school," says Jones. "Someone would say something to her, and before they could get another word out, she'd punch them." Chelsea was still enrolled in school, but she wasn't doing much better. Jones would drop her off at school on his way to work, only to have his wife call saying she had walked right back home.

CRIME AND PUNISHMENT

In January 2003, the twins pleaded guilty and were sentenced to a maximum of four years at a juvenile detention center in Bordentown, New Jersey. Now they live with 46 other girls ages 14 to 20 and attend school five days a week. There is also a salon where inmates can receive cosmetology training. Although the twins aren't roommates, they see each other all the time. Even so, their stepsister Danelle is certain that Chelsea and Elysia are homesick and want their freedom. But Detective Sergeant Duffy and Supervising Assistant Prosecutor Paulhus are confident that the sisters are better off in the detention center. "When two 14-year-old children rob a bank," says Paulhus, "you have to look to their parents for fault. The best thing that ever happened to those children was getting caught." Paulhus believes the girls got into this trouble in the first place because they were worried about losing their home. "Now they have a warm, dry place to sleep; plenty to eat; and they're getting an education," Paulhus says Duffy has been to see the girls a couple of times, and during a recent visit he found Chelsea happily cornrowing hair in the prison salon. She's resumed her Bible studies and recently sent a letter to her friend Tiffany vowing to create a positive future. "When I go home, the things I want to do will be through God," she wrote. "I want to live my life. It took getting locked up for me to realize that, but it's true."

Elysia is making her mark in other ways. In a hallway at the detention center are two large wall murals filled with messages of success and perseverance. The artist signed them "EW": Elysia Wortman.

LIFE TODAY

As for their parents, Jones went on trial this past September. He faced a maximum of 50 years for his crimes, including covering up the robbery and endangering the children. Jones eventually accepted a plea bargain of five years in prison for receiving stolen money and hindering apprehension of his family. He will be sentenced and sent to prison in January.

The twins testified against their stepfather in exchange for a reduced sentence. During her testimony, Elysia looked at him and said, "I'm mad at him and my mom for getting me into this situation." Kathleen pleaded guilty to armed robbery and using her children in a crime. She was sentenced to 15 years in New Jersey's state prison for women. She can't be paroled until 2016, when she has served 13 years of her sentence. And until her daughters are released, in 2007 or sooner (due in part to their testimony against their stepfather), her only contact with the twins will be by mail.

In the end, the Jones family lost the house Chelsea and Elysia wanted to save so badly. And all of their siblings are now separated—some living in foster homes and others with relatives. "I struggled so hard to keep my family together against all odds," says Jones. "We'd come so far, and then in 15 minutes, 14 years of struggle was destroyed."

the woman who seduced teenage boys

Guys liked to hang out at Kristin's* house because her mom, Silvia, let them drink. But the 40-year-old wanted sex in return...

Jon had been drunk and had passed out. The 17-year-old Arvada, Colorado, high school senior was lying on the floor when he woke up. He'd been hanging out in his friend Kristin's house after a typical school day in fall 2003, and he and several friends, mostly other guys from Arvada West High School, had been drinking shots of peppermint Schnapps, Goldschläger, and beer. Jon didn't know exactly how much alcohol he'd consumed, but he knew it was a lot.

As Jon was lying there he felt a tug, like someone was undressing him. He realized that was exactly what was happening: Someone was beside him, pulling off his clothes. But who was it? Kristin, 15, had a boyfriend. Then he saw who the person was: Silvia Johnson— Kristin's mother.

SUBURBAN MOM

Since the early '90s, Mrs. Johnson had lived on a tidy cul-de-sac in Arvada, just outside of Denver, with her

*Names have been changed.

71

husband, Jeff, and their three kids—Kristin and her two younger siblings. On the surface Mrs. Johnson didn't appear very different from any other suburban middle-class mom. "Whenever I saw her around the neighborhood, she always seemed nice, and she spent a lot of time with her children," says her next-door neighbor, Dorrel Bowler. "For years, she organized the neighborhood Easter-egg hunt."

Mrs. Johnson had felt like an outsider in high school, although the locals in Arvada generally considered her to be friendly and outgoing. But she also talked really fast, often blurting everything out at once; neighbors said she could be rambling and erratic. "She always seemed hyper," says Mr. Bowler, "like she was in a rush to get somewhere." He just assumed she had a lot on her mind.

By the summer of 2003, Mr. Bowler noticed that Mr. and Mrs. Johnson were fighting a lot—more frequently than most husbands and wives he knew. "Through their window I could hear them screaming and yelling," he says. "The neighbors called the police a few times." Sometime around then, Mr. Johnson moved out. He later filed for divorce.

PARTY TIME

One afternoon, about two months after Mr. Johnson moved out, Kristin's boyfriend, Gus,* 16, and several of his guy friends went over to Kristin's after school. When they got there, Mrs. Johnson stayed in the living room, talking and joking with them as if she were their age—even giving them shots of tequila.

That afternoon Mrs. Johnson sat between Jon and Rex,* 15. As they all drank, she began touching them while she was talking, flirting with each of them. The two guys thought it was weird that she was acting like one of the group and coming on to them—but no one else's mom would let them get drunk, so they went along with it. Kristin didn't seem to care that her mom was hanging out either. When the guys left that night, Mrs. Johnson told them to come back soon—and they were excited that they'd found a new place to drink and party.

The guys stopped by Kristin's again a week or so later, and this time Mrs. Johnson offered to drive to the liquor store to buy them all beer and a bottle of Jack Daniel's whiskey. After she returned home, she came on to several of the guys, like she had with Jon and Rex the week before. Mrs. Johnson's flirting creeped them out a bit, but they also figured that the free alcohol was more than worth putting up with it.

So the guys quickly got into a routine: Every few weeks they would go over to Mrs. Johnson's (sometimes with their girlfriends) to drink and party, and Mrs. Johnson, glad to have a chance to be the "cool mom," often gave them alcohol. By November the partying had gotten even *more* serious when the guys discovered that Mrs. Johnson had methamphetamine, a stimulant, stashed in her bathroom. She offered some to them and to Kristin, and even showed them how to snort it through a rolled-up dollar bill.

Around this time, Mrs. Johnson's neighbors started to notice that the same three or four cars were parked outside her home at least once a week, usually on weekend nights—and they saw the same young guys going in and out of the house. "I thought the guys were going over there to visit the daughter," Mr. Bowler says. He and the other neighbors were getting fed up with hearing loud music at night from the guys' car radios as they were coming and going. A couple of times Mr.

Bowler saw Mrs. Johnson during the afternoon, and he asked her what was going on. "She'd always say they were just good kids hanging out," he says.

FRIGHTENING TURN

As Jon lay naked on the floor that fall night, Mrs. Johnson climbed on top of him, kissing him and running her hands over his body. Jon was freaked out, but he'd never been in a situation like that before and didn't know what to do. She clearly wanted to have sex with him—but he wasn't into it. After all, this was his friend's *mom*. But he didn't say no, and Mrs. Johnson kept rubbing him. Then they had sex.

"She basically raped me," Jon said later. "There was no consent by me at all." A few weeks after the assault, Jon was hanging out with his best friend, Tim,* 16, who was also a regular at Mrs. Johnson's parties. Jon blurted out the whole story about what had happened: He told Tim that Mrs. Johnson had been all over him at the party—but that he'd been too drunk to know what he was doing.

Tim was surprised, but he wasn't shocked. Mrs. Johnson flirted a lot with the guys when they were drunk or high. No one complained about it—they didn't want the others to think they were lame. After all, they were guys—they were *supposed* to want sex, right? And if they stopped hanging out at Mrs. Johnson's, they wouldn't have a place to drink. Tim could tell his friend Jon was upset—as Tim recalled later, Jon "had tears in his eyes when he told me."

In an attempt to convince himself he wasn't upset, Jon continued to go to Mrs. Johnson's house. The parties went on for an entire year—throughout the rest of the school year and the summer. During those 12 months, Mrs. Johnson eventually had sex with five of the guys. Sometime during the summer, she even had sex once more with Jon after he'd again had too much to drink. And that was when everything changed—after that second time, Jon got sick of the scene at Mrs. Johnson's and stopped going to her parties. "I got tired of being around her. I got tired of being stupid and making bad decisions," Jon later said.

MAJOR CONFESSION

Jon spent the rest of the summer doing other things—since his friends were still going to Mrs. Johnson's, he didn't want to be around them. His mom was worried that his behavior had changed so drastically—he'd stopped dating and didn't seem interested in *anything*. But when she asked what was wrong, he just shrugged and said nothing.

By September 2004, one of the guys finally broke down—and told his mother about the drinking at Mrs. Johnson's parties. Furious, the mother contacted the police. At that time Mrs. Johnson was seeing a therapist, who told her the police *had* to be notified of what she'd done. Suspecting that she was facing serious trouble with the law, Mrs. Johnson decided to go talk to the cops.

So on an afternoon in October 2004, Kristin's mom walked into the Arvada Police Department. "I want to tell my side of the story," she told Detective Robert Vander Veen, who was handling the case. "I've been having parties where I've given minors alcohol—and had sex with them," she said.

Mrs. Johnson explained that she didn't really think she'd done anything wrong—she just wanted the guys to like her, she told the detective. Hanging out with

75

them made her feel like she finally belonged. "I was part of the group," she said. "I was a cool mom." She later explained that she thought if she had sex with these boys, she wouldn't get as emotionally attached to them as she might men her age. (She hoped to ultimately get back together with her ex-husband.) After talking to Detective Vander Veen, Mrs. Johnson drove home, where she waited to find out what crime she'd be charged with.

COURTROOM DRAMA

Mrs. Johnson was arrested on December 2, 2004—and on July 25, 2005, in a plea bargain with the district attorney, she pleaded guilty to nine counts of contributing to the delinquency of a minor (for serving drugs and alcohol to Kristin and the eight guys) and two counts of misdemeanor sexual assault.

Approximately a year after her arrest, on November 14, 2005, she appeared at her sentencing hearing. Her lawyer had hired a psychiatrist, Frederick Miller, M.D., as an expert witness. Dr. Miller diagnosed Mrs. Johnson with type 2 bipolar disorder, a condition that can cause hypersexual and irrational behavior, and which he said allowed her to think that what she was doing was okay. Through her tears, Mrs. Johnson apologized to the judge for her crimes.

The boys and their families attended the sentencing hearing, and many of the parents gave statements, calling Mrs. Johnson "perverted" and "narcissistic." As a result the judge sentenced her to a whopping 30 years in prison, which she is currently serving. "The sentence was so harsh because Mrs. Johnson showed no empathy to the victims until she cried in front of the judge," says Scott Storey, the district attorney who handled the sentencing.

Mrs. Johnson's attorney, Philip Cherner, thinks that her illness should warrant a lighter sentence. "She is mentally ill," he says. "Yes, she did serious damage to these kids, but she admitted it. She said she was sorry, and she's not an ongoing threat to the community." He is in the process of filing an appeal.

But Mr. Storey—and the victims—don't agree. "Mrs. Johnson sees herself as the victim [because of her mental illness]," says Mr. Storey.

And society may look at boys differently than girls in these sorts of cases, but make no mistake—these boys were victimized."

dying to get high

Mellie and Maria, both 18, were good students who were close to their families and friends. That's why everyone who knew them was so surprised by their tragic end.

Mariel Carballo was getting out of the shower around 6:30 P.M. on Friday, August 12, 2005, when the phone rang in her family's New York City apartment. The caller ID said it was Mellie, her 18-year-old daughter. "Hi, Melita," she answered. "Is this Mrs. Carballo?" a man's voice replied. Surprised, she demanded, "Who are you?" The caller said he was a policeman—he was calling from Cabrini Medical Center. "Is Mellie okay?!" Mrs. Carballo gasped. "It looks like she was drinking or doing drugs. Please come immediately." In a panic Mrs. Carballo threw on some clothes and ran outside to hail a cab.

FUN ONE

Mellie Carballo had always been very independent. Back in eighth grade she had told her Argentinean parents she didn't want to follow in her older sister Celeste's footsteps by going to the same high school. Mellie already shared a bunk bed and a closet with Celeste—and that was enough. So the Carballos decided that Mellie would go to St. Vincent Ferrer High School on Manhattan's East Side.

79

Mellie had a quirky sense of humor—she often talked with a fake Valley Girl accent—and quickly made a lot of friends at St. Vincent's. But she also got frustrated by the school's restrictive rules. So instead of wearing her uniform in the same way the rest of the students did, Mellie hemmed her skirt short and wore Guns N' Roses pins to stand out. During sophomore year she even pierced her tongue—which shocked her mom. But Mrs. Carballo thought it was just harmless teen rebellion.

During that same year Mellie started bonding with her classmate Maria Pesantez, a straight-A student from Jackson Heights, New York. Maria and Mellie were both into punk rock, especially The Clash, and wore band pins to school. "They loved to talk about music together and shop in the record stores in the Village," says Gina Apestegui, 19, one of their friends from St. Vincent's. Maria was definitely enamored of Mellie's edginess. "Mellie was the leader of her group in high school," recalls her sister, Celeste. "People always followed her and wanted to be like her." But unlike Mellie, Maria had strict Ecuadoran parents, an early curfew, and a *heavy* honors workload to help keep her wild side in check.

During her junior year, Mellie started going to hear music at downtown New York venues like CBGB. "Staying out late to dance is part of our culture," says her mom. "I thought she was enjoying her youth, like you're supposed to." But what Mrs. Carballo didn't know was that during her senior year, Mellie started snorting cocaine at some shows. People she knew were doing it—so Mellie thought it was no big deal.

BAD SCENE

After finishing high school, Mellie went to Hunter College in New York City, choosing to live at home to save money. During the day she took art history and psychology classes—but at night she was getting more and more in the club scene, where she'd listen to DJs, dance, and always meet new people. By the end of her first semester, Mellie was staying out until dawn a few nights a week—sometimes doing cocaine to stay energized. "She loved the club scene—the music, the fashion, the guys," says Ashley Benatar, 19, one of Mellie's friends from high school. "And she really liked how [drugs] made her feel," adds Valerie Ponelli, 17, another friend. "When Mellie was high she could dance all night and *then* go to an after-party starting at 5 A.M." Mellie felt like she had it all: cool friends, a tight-knit family, a good college—and a great party scene.

One Thursday night in June 2005, Mollie was at a party when an older guy introduced himself as KC. He seemed soft-spoken and sweet, and after the two talked for a bit, they left the party together. "She found out he was a dealer and figured he'd give her free cocaine because he liked her," a friend explains. Mellie was right: Over the next two months, KC sometimes gave her up to 15 grams of cocaine a week, and one of her friends says that Mellie's cocaine use got so intense that she would take various pills to come down from her cocaine high and get some sleep.

But even as Mellie's partying was spinning out of control, it seemed like she was still holding the reins. She was always on time, went to the gym three times a week, and didn't smoke or even drink coffee. "She acted like the same Mellie," Mrs. Carballo explains. "It was summer, and I knew she was having a good time with friends, but we still had breakfast together every day." The one thing Mrs. Carballo *did* notice was that Mellie was getting skinnier. "I did worry about how thin she was becoming," Mrs. Carballo recalls. "But I *never* considered that she could be addicted to drugs."

FATEFUL DAY

The week of August 7, 2005, Mellie was gearing up for that weekend's Warped Tour. She already had plans to see Saturday's show with friends—but she wanted to find someone to go with to Friday's concert. Mellie wasn't that close with Maria anymore, but she knew that Maria still loved the same music, so she called her Friday morning. "I'd love to go!" Maria said—and the girls decided to meet downtown a few hours later.

Around 9 A.M. Mellie had a bowl of cereal with her mom. "I'm going to the beach," Mellie lied, knowing her mom wouldn't want her partying *all* weekend. About a half hour later, Mellie left. "Have a safe trip," Mrs. Carballo said as she kissed her daughter goodbye.

Mellie got on the subway and headed downtown. Sometime before noon she met up with Maria—and KC, who introduced them to his friend Alfredo Morales. Then they all headed to Alfredo's apartment to party before Mellie and Maria went to the Warped Tour. Over the next few hours, Mellie, Maria, KC, and Alfredo are said to have listened to music and played Uno. They also reportedly drank alcohol and snorted eight bags of cocaine that may have been laced with heroin.

It soon became clear that Mellie and Maria had inhaled more drugs than their bodies could handle: At first they just seemed *really* out of it, but after a little while they began to convulse—and turn purple. Then Mellie passed out, and the guys started to panic, so they carried Maria's shaking body into the bathroom, hoping to stop her convulsions with cold water. But it didn't work. At around 6 P.M., about six hours after the girls had first arrived there, KC and Alfredo frantically dialed 911: "Send an ambulance to 484 East Houston Street!"

LOST HOPE

Mrs. Carballo's heart was racing as her cab sped to the hospital. "Mellie...what did you do?" she cried. A million thoughts raced through her head: Please let my baby be okay. I'm not strong enough for this. Mrs Carballo imagined Mellie lying in a bed very sick and scared, waiting for her family. When the driver pulled into the emergency entrance, Mrs. Carballo threw some money at him and ran in to the front desk.

"I'm Mellie Carballo's mom. Where is she?" she asked worriedly. A doctor stepped out from behind the desk and motioned Mrs. Carballo to follow him to an empty room. "We found Mellie unconscious. We tried..." he started. "What?! What are you saying?" Mrs. Carballo yelled. "Is she dead?!" Slowly the doctor nodded. Mrs. Carballo wailed in disbelief, "I need to see her!"

The doctor led Mrs. Carballo down the hall to a brightly lit room. She looked right past the nurses to Mellie, who was lying there with a tube coming out of her mouth—she looked like she was sleeping. Sobbing and shaking, Mrs. Carballo walked over to her daughter and hugged her, kissing her still-warm cheek. "Why?" Mrs. Carballo asked, weeping as she took Mellie's hand. "Who did this to you? What could I have done?" She was overcome with an emptiness she'd never felt before.

SHOCKING REALITY

For the next day Maria was unconscious at Bellevue, another local hospital—until she also died from acute cocaine and heroin intoxication. Maria and Mellie were laid to rest at separate funerals. "She was so alive," says

Ashley, a high school friend of Mellie's, who attended her funeral. "She thought nothing could happen to her—as did we."

On August 17, police arrested Alfredo Morales, 33— and charged him with selling cocaine to Mellie and Maria. Several days after that, KC—who actually turned out to be Roberto Martinez, 41, a member of a heroin-dealing gang called the Cut Throat Crew—was arrested for violating his parole and was sent to Willard Drug Treatment Campus in upstate New York. Morales was sentenced to five years in jail and five years probation.

Since Mellie's death, the Carballos are still trying to figure out how their daughter went from being a fun-loving, independent girl to a tragic victim of the New York party scene. They blame Roberto and Alfredo for pressuring the girls to do too many drugs. Meanwhile, the Pesantez family has accused Mellie, without proof, of trying to recruit Maria to be a customer for Roberto. (Friends say Maria used cocaine several times before the night she died.) But blame won't bring either girl back, and Mrs. Carballo is left wishing she'd known about Mellie's drug problem. "I knew her friends wanted to be loyal—but if only they'd told me," she whimpers. "Now my entire world has come to an end."

girl still missing

One cold winter night, Maura, 21, just picked up and left her college campus—and vanished without a trace.

Route 112 near Haverhill, New Hampshire, has lots of twists and turns, but none are quite as wicked as the 90-degree swerve across from the Weathered Barn, a dilapidated former antiques store. And at 7:30 P.M. on February 9, 2004, Maura Murray, 21, found out just how difficult it can be to navigate that turn—when she completely missed it.

Maura's '96 Saturn careened off the road into the woods, barely missing a tree. She was fine. The car wasn't. The radiator was damaged, and the wheels sank into a few feet of packed snow. About five minutes later, a school bus drove by. Butch Atwood, the driver, was off-duty and headed to his cabin just up the road. "Are you okay?" he shouted to Maura in her car. "Should I call AAA?"

Maura rolled down her window and shivered from the 12-degree chill. She mumbled that she'd already called AAA for a tow. Atwood thought she seemed like she'd been drinking. "Okay," he said, "I'll call the police and fire department. Why don't you come to my house? You can get warm and wait there."

"No," Maura replied firmly, "I'll wait here."

Atwood thought it was possible that Maura might

have been scared of him—he weighs 350 pounds and has a grizzled beard—so he didn't press the point. Instead, he drove the 100 yards to his cabin and called the police himself. About 15 minutes later, Atwood saw the police pull up to Maura's car.

When they looked inside, they found an open can of Skyy Blue malt liquor in the front seat. In the back was a suitcase filled with clothes; a stuffed monkey and a diamond necklace that her boyfriend, Bill Rausch, had given to her; two textbooks; and another book—*Not Without Peril*, an account of people who died climbing New Hampshire's Mount Washington, bookmarked at a chapter titled "A Question of Life or Death."

But Maura was nowhere in sight.

TAKING OFF

No one knows where Maura was going three hours earlier when she got into her car at the University of Massachusetts at Amherst, where she was a junior studying nursing. She didn't tell her friends, her family, or her boyfriend that she was leaving campus at all. The only thing she said to Bill, in an e-mail she'd sent at 1 P.M. that day (after she'd failed to return his two phone calls and an e-mail he sent the previous day) was, "i love you more stud. i got your messages, but honestly, i didn't feel like talking to much of anyone, i promise to call today though. Love you." Four hours after she e-mailed Bill, Maura *did* write a note to her boss at the campus art gallery before she took off.

In it, she said that she had a family emergency and had to go out of town for a week. According to the police report, she had also checked out information about Stowe Mountain and printed out directions to

Burlington, Vermont (which is in the opposite direction from where she'd crashed). Then she packed her stuff, left her dorm, took $280 out of an ATM, bought a can of Skyy Blue and a bottle of red wine at a liquor store, got in her car—and started driving.

EARLY WARNING

Maura had always seemed like she had it all together. She was ranked fourth in her high school class (she scored a 1420 on her SAT), and enrolled at the U.S. Military Academy at West Point. Then, in fall 2003, Maura transferred to UMass Amherst because she decided she'd rather heal people than kill them, says her father, Fred Murray.

Maura had always shown athletic prowess too, and in high school her reputation as a star runner (she ran a five-minute mile) was known throughout Massachusetts. But when Maura didn't win a race, which was rare, she'd get really quiet. Even though you could tell she was beating herself up inside for not winning, if you asked her whether she was upset, she'd shake her head no. Maura was like that: She kept things to herself and few people ever saw her cry.

That is, until a few days before she disappeared. Four days earlier, on Thursday, February 5, Maura had called her older sister Kathleen, 26, at around 10:20 P.M., during a quiet patch at Maura's second job manning a dorm security desk. "I was telling her all about this fight I'd had with my fiancé," says Kathleen. "Maura kept saying, 'Don't worry, he's a good guy. It'll work out.'" After they got off the phone, Maura was sitting at her desk doing her job. Then, according to police reports, she inexplicably burst into tears in front of a coworker—and wouldn't say why.

ANOTHER OUTBURST

Two days later, on Saturday, February 7, Maura's dad drove up to Amherst to help Maura buy a new car. Maura and her father spent the day at car dealerships and then hit the Amherst Brewing Company for grilled chicken salads. At 10 P.M. her dad wanted to call it a night, so he had Maura drop him off at his motel, then drive herself to the dorm in his car.

About an hour later, Maura arrived at her friend Sara Alfieri's dorm room to hang out. For the next three hours, Maura, Sara, and a couple of friends sat around talking and listening to music while drinking Skyy Blue malt mixed with a little bit of wine. A couple of times, when there were pauses in the conversation, Maura mentioned that she wanted to return the car to her dad that night. "It didn't make any sense," says Kate Markopolous, who was there. Why would Maura, who'd had a few drinks and seemed tired, go to the trouble of driving all the way to her dad's motel in the middle of the night, when she didn't need to?

At 2:30 A.M., Maura left Sara's room, telling everyone she was going to go upstairs to her room. But instead, she got in her dad's car and started driving back to his motel. On the highway, the car jumped a sandy embankment and hit a guardrail. The front of the car's radiator crumpled, so Maura called AAA to tow the car. The police arrived and wrote up a report—but didn't give Maura a ticket.

When Maura told her father about the accident the next morning, he was upset. "The first thing I asked was, 'Are you all right?'" he says. As Fred Murray called garages, Maura sat there crying. "She kept repeating 'I'm sorry' over and over," he says. "I think she felt like she had really let me down." At 2 P.M., Murray dropped a still-teary Maura off at her dorm in a rental car. "I said, 'Maura, it will get fixed. Don't worry,'" he says. Then Maura got out, and her dad drove away.

DESPERATE SEARCH

The next day, on February 9, the New Hampshire police arrived at the scene of Maura's second accident—the one on Route 112. The police, fire department, and local residents searched area roads for her. They also left a message for the Murray family to let them know that there had been an accident. When Maura didn't turn up the next day, the police called again and told them she was missing.

Fred Murray drove up to New Hampshire and got a room at the Wells River Motel, near the accident site. As the police continued their search, Murray, along with the rest of his family and Maura's boyfriend, combed the area too. "I can't explain how it feels to be walking up an embankment, thigh-deep in snow, and then there's a big hill in front of you, and you have to walk up it because you see footprints in the snow and you might find your sister's body at the end," says Kathleen.

Two days after Maura's disappearance, dogs had tracked her scent to the road, about 100 yards away from the site. Her family thought that maybe someone had picked Maura up, so they printed up 15,000 flyers with her picture, and a crew of volunteers began tacking them to every signpost and gas station within 50 miles. But weeks went by, and no one came forward. So the Murrays are still searching for Maura.

QUESTIONS REMAIN

There is still no sign of Maura. "The only thing that makes sense is that a bad guy got her," says her dad.

89

But police disagree. "There is no evidence that she was abducted," says New Hampshire State Police Sergeant Thomas Yorke. Police have told newspapers that they suspect Maura intended to kill herself, but they've reached no conclusions. "As far as we're concerned, she's a missing person," says Yorke.

Maura's crying, along with her atypical drinking (her family and friends say she wasn't a drinker) and the two car accidents just before she disappeared, raises the question of whether she was buckling under some emotional pain. "I don't know what could have been going on that she didn't tell me about," says Bill. "As far as I knew, everything was fine."

"I may go to my grave never knowing where she's gone or even why she left school," says her father. "And as far as I can tell, no one else knows either."

natural born killers

When Tiffany was 12, she fell in love with
19-year-old Tony. Their parents tried to keep them
apart—so the couple did the unthinkable.

A bout a month before Christmas in 2003, Tiffany Khauv, a 12-year-old from San Jose, California, was typing up her wish list: Old Navy cardigan ($18), low-rider Dickies ($38), and a heart necklace ($275). Next to the necklace, she wrote, "reserved for Tony," so Anthony "Tony" Chargualaf, her 19-year-old boyfriend, would know to buy it. It was obvious that Tony was willing to make Tiffany happy—at any cost.

LONELY HEART

Tiffany, a seventh-grader at Piedmont Middle School, was a mostly A student and sang in the choir. She had lots of friends and lived with her mom, her 17-year-old brother, and her grandparents. But on Friday, October 10, 2003, Tiffany sat down at her computer and wrote in her online diary: "The way I'm feeling is horrible."

Tiffany was beginning to spend a lot of time on the Internet and phone—and less time with her family. "I always have the feeling that I'm not wanted," she wrote. But her mom didn't realize that—and she was getting annoyed with Tiffany for choosing to keep to herself so much. On Sunday, October 19, Tiffany was on the phone with a friend, as usual, when her mom finally

91

yanked out the cord. "Who's so important?!" she demanded to know. Tiffany thought to herself, Just because
you don't have a life, you don't have to ruin mine!

FORBIDDEN LOVE

One day in mid-October, Tiffany was at the mall when
some friends introduced her to Tony, a cashier they
knew at CyberHunt, an Internet café where they all
hung out. Tony was a lonely kid, just like Tiffany.

He'd spent most of his youth shuttling back and forth
between his father near Tacoma, Washington, and his
mother in Milpitas, California, where he was now
living. After Tony and Tiffany met, the two started
e-mailing and chatting online. By November, they were
calling each other boyfriend and girlfriend. But
Tiffany's mom forbade them to have a relationship
because of their big age difference. Still, as often as
possible, they'd meet at the mall. Tony even came to
Tiffany's school to see her between classes.

In May, Tiffany had a school trip to Six Flags Magic
Mountain, and Tony met her there—it was a unique
chance for them to spend the whole day together. But
when chaperones noticed him hugging Tiffany, they
reported it to the principal, who notified Tiffany's mom.

A few nights later, Tiffany heard her mom talking to
her aunt, saying she wanted Tony in jail. After snoop-
ing, her mom had found some pictures of the couple
kissing, which might help prove Tony's illegal relationship with her underage daughter. Panicked, Tiffany
immediately contacted Tony. "Let's run away!" she said.

GROWING DESPERATION

Terrified that he and Tiffany might be separated, Tony
stole his mom's credit card, bought two plane tickets to

Hawaii, and they took off. Tiffany's mom noticed her daughter was gone and reported her missing. But it wasn't until four days later that Tony's mom tracked them down on his cell. "What's going on?" she asked. "We ran away," he replied. Then he said he was so desperate to be with Tiffany that they were going to jump off a mountain so they could die together.

Upon hearing that, Tony's mom hung up, horrified, and called the Hawaii police department. Using information from her credit-card bill, they busted Tony and Tiffany in their hotel room a few hours later. "Pack your bags," an officer said. "You won't be coming back."

Later that night, Tiffany was sent against her will to her mom in California. Tony was held in a Hawaiian jail until he was released a few days later, in early June, pending investigation for child rape. Once he got back home, he was scared that the police would charge him—and he'd lose Tiffany for good. So together they made a new plan. The next Saturday morning, Tony stole his stepdad's Toyota truck, picked up Tiffany at her home, and they fled again—this time to Tony's father's home in University Place, Washington. Even though Tony's father, Anthony Chargualaf, had heard about Tony's illegal trip to Hawaii, he welcomed the pair and set up a mattress for them in his living room.

But for some reason, Tony didn't reciprocate his father's generosity. Later that week he stole his father's credit cards and took Tiffany shopping for new clothes and a haircut. Within hours, Chargualaf's credit-card company called him, asking about unusual activity.

Later that evening, Tony spoke to his father on the phone. "Get over here and get your stuff!" Chargualaf screamed. He knew that Tony had stolen from him— and he wanted him out. When Tony arrived, his father had already piled up all his clothes. "Give me my key," Chargualaf said coldly. Knowing full well why his father was so mad, Tony simply handed it over and left.

Over the next few days, Tony's other relatives from the area let the couple stay with them, not realizing how young Tiffany was. But then Tony's uncle told him that Chargualaf was planning to call the police and report that his son was dating a minor. So once again, Tony panicked. He knew that he had to stop his father—or risk losing the love of his life. So at 2 P.M. on June 25, he and Tiffany drove to his father's home.

NECESSARY EVIL

While Tiffany waited down the street in the truck, Tony pried open his father's window and entered the empty apartment. He brought two knives with him, but he also looked around the apartment for more—and found a machete to place by his side.

After about an hour of silently waiting in the living room, Tony heard his father's footsteps on the gravel outside, approaching the apartment. As the door opened, Tony kept his two knives in his pockets. Chargualaf spotted his son—and immediately began yelling at him. "What are you doing?!" he screamed. "You're dating a 13-year-old!" Suddenly wild with anger, Tony pulled out one of the knives and lunged toward his father, stabbing him in the neck.

Chargualaf began bleeding as he tried to fight back. He grabbed the machete that Tony had placed in the living room and used it to hit his son on top of the head. But then Tony grabbed his father's neck and started choking him—until Chargualaf managed to use the machete to cut a huge gash in his son's leg. But Tony was able to pry the weapon out of his father's hand—and began beating his dad over the head with it.

Within minutes, the two burst outside through the front door, where Tony continued to beat his father—until Chargualaf finally slumped over into a bush, twitching. As Tony watched his father take his last few breaths, he called down the street to Tiffany, "Babe?!"

She got out of the truck and walked toward them, where she saw Tony—and his father's body—covered in blood. Tiffany says she was shocked—yet she didn't flee. Instead she stood by. Tony dragged Chargualaf inside. "Can you help me clean the house?" Tony asked Tiffany. "Yeah," she said, cringing.

Likely in shock over what they'd just done, they took a few days to buy cleaning supplies, plastic storage bins, and an electric saw that Tony planned to use to cut the body into pieces before disposing it in the plastic bins. That week after the murder, they had dinner together at a Red Robin—where Tony finally broke down. "I feel bad about killing my dad," he said quietly. Tiffany looked down at her hamburger and was reminded of the rancid smell of blood in the house. She felt like she was going to throw up.

On July 1, the odor in Chargualaf's home got so bad that Gerard Sullivan, an owner of the chiropractic office above the apartment, called the landlord. After the two men decided to let themselves into the empty apartment, Sullivan noticed plastic wrapping piled by the front door. Slowly he lifted it—and found the rotting corpse, which the kids still hadn't cut up. They immediately flagged down a police cruiser passing by.

Shortly after, Tiffany and Tony were on their way back to Chargualaf's home when they spotted the police car out front. Panicked once again, they drove past the building without stopping. They had nowhere left to go, so they randomly decided to drive to Florida. Six days later, as Tiffany and Tony were in a hotel in Missoula, Montana, on their way east, police, after tracking them by their credit-card purchases, arrested them.

LASTING CONSEQUENCES

Tony and Tiffany were brought to the local police station, where Tony confessed to the murder. "Did you go with the idea that you wanted a confrontation with your dad?" detectives asked. "I didn't want it to happen, but then, like, in order to be with Tiffany, yeah," he said. Detectives interviewed Tiffany separately. "Did you ever think about calling 911?" they asked. "Yeah . . . but I was kind of a runaway, so I would get in trouble and I was frightened," she said. Then she asked, "I can't see [Tony]?" The answer was a resounding no.

After spending 15 days in juvenile detention, Tiffany was sent home to her mom in San Jose, where she stayed until her September 27 sentencing hearing for providing criminal assistance to Tony. Her eyes darted nervously as her lawyer coached her through her statement. "I apologize for all the mistakes I've done," she said quickly. Then the judge sentenced her to 15 more days in a juvenile detention center.

Meanwhile Tony remained in jail, where he pleaded guilty to first-degree murder and second-degree child rape. On October 15, 2004, he was sentenced to serve 285 months in prison—more than 23 years. "I just wish it never happened," he told investigators. "Did you love your dad?" they asked. "Yes," he replied. "But the reason this happened is because that love for Tiffany was the most important thing?" they pressed, in hopes of understanding his motive. "Yeah," he said. But now, as Tiffany resumes her life—going to 8th grade, even meeting new boys—she is forbidden by law to have any contact with Tony. And Tony just sits alone behind bars, paying for his heinous crime of passion.

josh's suicide

When Josh, 20, began pulling away from his tight-knit family, they had no idea that he was heading toward a tragic end.

About 9 P.M. on Sunday, June 13, 2004, Jodi Bergkamp, 20, was watching TV at her home in Norfolk, Virginia. She picked up the phone to call her parents in Branson, Missouri, as she did every night before bed. "It's me," Jodi casually said when her mom, Carolyn Horne, answered. "I can't talk. There are people here," her mom abruptly replied—and hung up.

Jodi was confused—her mom *always* had time to talk to her. What was going on? Finally, 10 minutes later, her phone rang. Figuring it must be her mom, she ran over to get it. "Hello?!" Jodi asked. But all she heard was soft crying on the other end. It was her older brother Tony, and he had to talk to her about her twin brother, Josh.

GOOD BOY

Jodi and Josh grew up on a farm in Ottawa, Kansas, with their parents, two older brothers, and younger sister. They were all close and spent a lot of time together but in many ways, Josh was the center of it all. He was the comedian—making everyone laugh with his "happy kick dance" and the celebrity imitations he did around the house.

Josh was also known as the handsome one—and he was proud of that. "He spent more time [primping] in the bathroom than his sisters," says his dad, Dan Horne. "I guess it paid off, considering he always had a girlfriend." Josh spent a great deal of time perfecting his sports too, especially cross-country running. In March 1997, when Josh was 14, he announced he wanted to spend his spring break running across Kansas—more than 200 miles. For seven days, the family slowly drove behind Josh as he completed his goal. "We thought he was crazy," says Jodi. "But he was so proud when he finished. The papers wrote about him—we thought he'd be in the Olympics one day."

FALLING STAR

By the time Josh was 16 and a junior in high school, he was the top runner at his school—but he began to feel overwhelmed by pressure from his coach to win every meet. After school one fall day, he simply told his dad, "Running isn't fun anymore." And he quit, just like that.

Not wanting his son to feel more pressure, Mr. Horne didn't say anything. But within weeks of leaving the team, Josh, who'd always had trouble keeping up his grades, began cutting classes. Then one day, about two months before the end of his junior year, he came home from school and told his parents, "I'm not going back."

Even though they knew Josh had been having a rough year, his parents were shocked and upset. But they knew their son: When he set his mind to do something—like running across Kansas—they couldn't change it. So after days of trying to persuade him to at least finish the semester, Mr. Horne agreed to let Josh get his GED instead.

Josh began working odd jobs, like pulling hay on farms. He also began staying out late with some new friends—other dropouts he'd met hanging around town. One night, about a month after Josh quit school, he came home at midnight to find his dad awake. "You've been drinking?" Mr. Horne bluntly asked when he smelled alcohol on his son. "I just took a sip from a friend," Josh said nervously—he knew alcohol was forbidden in his Christian home. Wanting to believe that his son wasn't breaking any rules, Mr. Horne simply said, "Don't do it again," and sent Josh to bed. But just three weeks later, Mr. Horne heard Josh come home at 1 A.M.—and throw up. The next morning, he pulled Josh aside. "Liquor is going to get ahold of you if you're not careful," he sternly warned his son.

ROCK BOTTOM

By the time Josh turned 19, he had lost touch with his school friends—and was still staying out late with the new friends he'd made. One day in June 2002, right after his 19th birthday, Mrs. Horne got an urgent call from one of the new friends: "Josh just got into an argument—someone's after him," she quickly said. "He's going to your house." When Josh showed up, he smelled of alcohol and had a glazed, almost crazed look in his eyes. Once inside, he began pacing back and forth and cursing his mom and brother Tony. "F*** you!" he screamed. Recently, Josh had been losing his temper—but he'd never been this out of control. Frightened and confused, Mrs. Horne began crying. Suddenly, Tony turned to her. "Tell the hospital we're coming," he said. Then he tackled Josh onto the couch and told him, "You're going for some treatment." At first Josh tried to get free, but after a few minutes he just went limp and mumbled, "Okay." Tony then helped Josh into their truck. As Tony drove, Josh laid his head down on his big brother's leg and sobbed.

Two weeks later, Josh was released from the hospital's alcohol-treatment program and went home. For a few months, he stayed out of trouble. He and his 27-year-old brother, Jonnie, even thought it would be fun if they moved in together, so Josh went to live with Jonnie. But around 12 A.M. one night in October 2002, about four months after Josh was let go from the hospital, Jonnie heard a commotion out front. So he got up, walked outside—and saw Josh getting handcuffed. He was being arrested for drunk driving. "I'm so sorry, Jonnie!" Josh called out, and he began to cry.

DESPERATE INTERVENTION

The next day Mr. Horne went to bail his son out of jail. He couldn't overlook it any longer: Josh's drinking was just getting worse. "You need to go to a real rehab," he told his son. "I'll take you anywhere for help." But now sober, Josh seemed to forget his regret from the previous night and completely denied having a problem. Since Josh was legally an adult and no longer living at home, Mr. Horne didn't feel he had the power to force his son to go get help.

By April 2004, a year and half later, Josh moved in with his girlfriend of four months, Cynthia, 20, and her baby, Jared. Shortly after, two of Josh's friends were at his place drinking, when one began flirting with Cynthia. Josh got really angry and demanded that they leave. As they walked out, one guy threw a garbage can through Josh's patio window. Fuming, Josh started yelling and raced out after them. When he caught up with them, the guys smashed Josh's eye socket and cheekbone, and knocked out his two front teeth.

Josh spent the next week in the hospital under observation for his head injuries. When he got out, his parents, who'd moved three hours away to Branson, Missouri, urged Josh to stay with them while he recovered. "Okay," Josh agreed, "I just want to get away from everybody." Josh was still pretty vain, so he grew a goatee to help cover his scabs and stitches, and his parents offered to replace his teeth once he healed. Until then, Josh hid his gap by rarely smiling. "I can't stand looking like this," he told his mom. The only thing that seemed to cheer him up was finding out that his girlfriend, Cynthia, was pregnant—the two started talking about marriage.

On Sunday, June 13, 2004, a few weeks after leaving the hospital, Josh's parents decided to spend the afternoon looking for a car to buy Josh. He'd just gotten a job at a gas station and needed a way to get to work. "Want to come?" Mr. Horne asked. "Nah," Josh replied. "I'm going to watch a movie." A half hour later, Jodi, Josh's twin, called. "What are you doing?" she asked. "Looking in the phone book for a club," he said. "I'm so bored. If I don't find something to do soon, I'm going to put a noose around my neck."

LOST HOPE

After a few hours of car shopping, Josh's parents pulled into their driveway at 7:30 P.M. They saw Josh in a white T-shirt and blue shorts, sitting against the garage wall. His head was slumped forward and his eyes were closed. "What the hell?" Mr. Horne asked, as he got out of the car and began walking toward his son. Suddenly, he stopped. There was an extension cord hanging from a rafter—and the other end was wrapped tightly around Josh's neck.

Mrs. Horne was standing near her husband and yelled Josh's name. Mr. Horne sprinted to his son and screamed out for his wife to call 911. He tried to relax the cord's tight hold but couldn't. "Get me a knife!" he shouted to Mrs. Horne, who was now inside, sobbing into the phone: "My baby boy hung himself! You need to send someone!" Then Mrs. Horne hung up and ran back to the garage with a knife. Mr. Horne grabbed the knife and frantically sawed away at the cord until in snapped. Once it did, Josh's limp body fell forward into his father's arms.

"Open your eyes, Josh," Mrs. Horne cried. "He can't be dead!" But as Mr. Horne held Josh tightly, he knew his son was gone—and he began to cry too. Then he looked down and saw a folded note in Josh's waistband. What if I've done something to cause this, he wondered. He didn't want to know if he had, so he left the note where it was.

MISSED OPPORTUNITIES

On June 17, the day before Josh's funeral, Jodi had her 21st birthday—without her twin. "I didn't want a cake," she says. "I felt so guilty for not taking his threat seriously."

For three months, no one in the family read Josh's note; the police had it. But when they gave it back, Mr. Horne finally opened it. "I did what I did because I was weak," Josh had explained. "I couldn't handle life." But today, a year after the suicide, Mr. Horne blames himself. "I let Josh down," he says. "I just hoped that he'd go back to his old self. I never realized that everything—his change of friends, his mood swings— were cries for help."

angel
of death

When Michele, 18, had a fight with
her dad, she had no idea it would be the
last time she'd see him alive.

It was 3:30 P.M. on a Sunday when Michele, then 16,
got the call. She'd been lounging around, watching
TV at her home in South Plainfield, New Jersey. It
was her cousin who worked at a nearby hospital, on
the line: "I'm not sure," her cousin blurted out, "but I
saw a guy who looked like your dad being brought into
the emergency room." Shocked and confused, Michele
mumbled, "Thanks," hung up, and immediately told her
mom, Janette. "It's not Daddy, right?!" Michele asked,
panicking, as her mom frantically dialed the hospital.
But as soon as Janette got through, she was told that
Chris Hardgrove, Michele's 38-year-old dad, *was* in the
hospital—in the critical care unit, in a coma.

DADDY'S GIRL

When Michele was young, she was very close to her
father. "I was the apple of my dad's eye," she says. He
would build her dollhouses, and they'd watch cartoons
together, but her favorite pastime was simply hanging
out and listening to her dad play the drums. "I'd
squeeze inside the bass as he'd bang away," she says.

Then in 2001, when Michele was 15, her parents got
divorced. Within a year, her dad moved in with his

girlfriend. "She'd try to start trouble between me and my dad," Michele says. "She'd say things like, 'Your dad wants to disown you.' And for some reason, I believed her, so I was too scared to say anything back."

One day in the summer of 2002, before Michele's sophomore year of high school, she went to visit her dad. "He started throwing accusations at me," she says. "He said he'd 'heard' that I'd started smoking and doing drugs—but it wasn't true! He'd also heard through my grandmother that I'd gotten my belly button pierced, which he wasn't happy about."

"I didn't defend myself," continues Michele. "But when I left, I thought, I don't have to deal with this—and we stopped talking." Even though they'd been speaking less since the divorce, this was a drastic change. That Christmas, Michele's dad sent her a card like he had the year before, signed, "Love, Daddy," with $100 in it. But *this* time she didn't call to thank him. "I was still angry," she says. "But he was my dad. I assumed the fight would just fizzle, and we'd make up."

SECOND CHANCE?

When Michele found out that her dad was in the hospital, she hadn't spoken to him in a year. But right away, she and her mom, Janette, rushed down to see him at Somerset Medical Center. Holding Janette's hand, Michele walked into her dad's room—and burst into tears. She couldn't believe how pale and fragile he looked. Soon a nurse came in and told them that his girlfriend had found him at home unconscious that morning. Paramedics were eventually able to resuscitate him, but he still wasn't breathing on his own. Doctors believed he'd had a massive heart attack.

Michele and her mom were speechless. "Chris had always been so healthy and strong," says Janette. "He was only 38—he'd never had any health problems."

After the nurse left, Janette hugged Michele tightly and said, "You need to make peace with your dad in case he doesn't pull through this. Do you want a few minutes alone with him?" Michele hesitantly nodded.

At first Michele stood a foot away from her dad's bed. "His breathing sounded so forced," Michele says. But after a few minutes, she stepped closer and put her hand on top of his, hoping he'd squeeze back to let her know he was okay. But he didn't. "I had so many thoughts in my head that I couldn't get any words out," she says. "I felt so guilty for not having spoken to him before this. Now I was scared I'd never get the chance."

At 11 that night, after they were back at home, Janette called the hospital to find out how Chris was doing. Although he was still in serious condition, his body was functioning—and he hadn't gotten any worse.

SUDDEN GOOD-BYE

At 6 the next morning, Janette called the hospital again to see if Chris's condition had changed. She spoke to a male nurse who'd been monitoring Chris through the night. "He went into cardiac arrest several times during the night," he said. "Should I come down?!" Janette shrieked. "I probably would," he replied.

Janette rushed there. When she got to Chris's room, things were eerily calm. The male nurse she'd spoken to had left, but the nurse on duty told Janette that Chris wasn't doing well: The medication to regulate his blood pressure was at the maximum dosage, but it wasn't helping enough, and his organs were shutting down. His kidneys had already stopped functioning, and his liver was failing. Janette looked over at Chris and saw a stream of blood begin to run out of his nose.

Moments later, a doctor strode in, and admitted to Janette that they weren't feeling positive about what was going on. "In my opinion, the best thing would be to take Chris off life support," she said, explaining that due in part to his failing organs, Chris was most likely brain-dead—and would remain in a coma forever.

After much deliberation, Chris's family agreed that they should take him off the blood-pressure medicine that was keeping him alive. Within five minutes of doing that—just 24 hours after he was first admitted to the hospital—Chris's heart stopped beating.

SERIOUS SUSPICIONS

When Janette got home from the hospital, Michele was sleeping on the couch. She sat down and stroked her hair to wake her. "Daddy's gone," Janette whispered. Michele rolled away and began quietly crying. She thought to herself, But we were supposed to make up!

In the months that followed, Michele began her junior year and tried not to think about her dad—she wanted life to feel normal again. But then in December 2003, four months after her dad's death, Michele was in homeroom when she saw a local paper, the *Courier News*, on a nearby desk. It had a big, intriguing headline that said "Angel of Death," so she picked it up. She skimmed the story and saw that it was about a nurse named Charles Cullen who had been accused of murdering a patient at Somerset Medical Center, where he'd worked between September 2002 and October 2003.

The article said he'd used a medication to perform what he called a "mercy killing" to alleviate the patients' suffering. Michele realized, That's when Dad was there! For a second she even wondered if maybe Cullen had anything to do with her father's death—but then thought, Something that outrageous wouldn't happen to us.

A few days later, Michele was watching TV when another story about Cullen came on. He admitted that he'd killed about 15 other patients at Somerset. That's when it occurred to Michele there was an *actual* possibility that this monster had killed her dad. She called her mom at work: "Do you think it's possible that this Angel of Death nurse had anything to do with Daddy?" she asked. "Well," Janette said, "I've already called prosecutors with your father's information."

FINAL CONFRONTATION

Four months later, in April 2004, the prosecutor's office called Janette at work. "You were right," a detective told her. "Charles Cullen admitted to murdering Christopher Hardgrove." He then told her that Cullen would be appearing in court two days later, to formally plead guilty to her ex-husband's murder, as well as to the murders of 13 other patients. The victims' families were allowed to attend.

As soon as Janette got home from work, she told Michele about the call. "We were right," she said. "The nurse said he was responsible for your dad's death." Michele just looked at her mom in shock and asked, "Why did he choose Dad?" Janette could only shake her head in despair as she answered, "I don't know."

At 10:30 A.M. on April 29, Michele, along with her mom, sister, and grandmother, sat anxiously in the front row of a packed courtroom in Somerville, New Jersey. A handcuffed Charles Cullen sat just five feet in front of them. "He didn't look like a murderer," says

Michele. "He had a Hawaiian shirt on." Michele held her mom's hand as she felt a growing nervousness inside. A few times she looked right at Cullen, to try and force him to see the pain he'd caused her, but he kept his eyes on the floor, as if he were ashamed.

The room was silent as Cullen's attorney began questioning him about each victim. When Michele heard her dad's name, she held her breath.

Lawyer: Count 11, with respect to Christopher Hardgrove, on or about August 11, 2003, at Somerset Medical, you had access to that patient?

Cullen: Yes.

Lawyer: And medication?

Cullen: Yes.

Lawyer: And you in fact injected that patient?

Cullen: Yes.

Lawyer: With the intent to cause his death?

Cullen: Yes.

Lawyer: And that medication was?

Cullen: Norepinephrine.

Lawyer: And in fact he did expire?

Cullen: Yes . . .

Then the trial moved on. "The part about my dad was so fast, it barely registered," Michele says, frustrated that she still doesn't know *why* Cullen had picked him.

"I still have so much guilt," Michele says today, nearly two years after her dad died. "I didn't have the courage to fix things when he was alive; now I'm going to have to live with that blame. But I also blame Cullen. He had *no* right to control my dad's fate—or mine."

killed for getting pregnant

Chelsea, 14, thought it was cool to date an older guy. But she never dreamed the relationship would result in her death.

At about 8 P.M. on Friday, June 9, 2006, Chelsea Brooks, 14, of Wichita, Kansas, was planning to secretly meet her ex-boyfriend, Elgin "Ray-Ray" Robinson Jr., who she called Ray. Chelsea, then nine months pregnant, was forbidden by her parents to see Ray, 20, because he was so much older—and because he was the one who had gotten her pregnant. So her friend Everett Gentry, 17, took her to see him. Everett dropped her off at his sister's house and told her he was going to get Ray and bring him there. But when Everett returned an hour later, he wasn't with Ray—he was with Ted Burnett, 49, a man Chelsea didn't know. Angry that Ray had stood her up, Chelsea demanded that Everett drive her back to the skating rink where her friends were waiting. He agreed, but said that first they had to drop Ted off somewhere. Chelsea climbed into the front passenger seat of Everett's car while Ted sat in the backseat right behind her.

Then, according to Everett's court testimony, as he drove east toward the edge of town, Ted took out an electronics cord and brutally yanked it around Chelsea's neck. While she struggled and kicked, Ted pulled the cord tighter. She tried to breathe, but within minutes she was dead.

DANGEROUS RELATIONSHIP

Chelsea was 10 years old when she first met Ray, then 16, through one of her best friends. In seventh grade, the girls played basketball at the YMCA, where Ray's father coached a youth basketball team (Ray was his assistant). Chelsea developed a crush on Ray, and when she was 12, she started calling him her boyfriend and put up a picture of him in her locker at Allison Middle School. Ray, who had dropped out of high school, worked as a dishwasher and was a part-time DJ at school parties and at weddings. Chelsea thought it was cool to date an older guy who had a job and bought gifts for her.

In July 2005, when she was only 13, Chelsea confided to her friend Amanda King* that she'd had sex with 19-year-old Ray. Amanda was shocked—and immediately told her mother, who called Chelsea's mom. But when Mrs. Brooks asked Chelsea if it was true, she denied it. Still, her mom forbade her to see Ray again, and called the police. Because Chelsea wouldn't admit to having sex with Ray, the police told her mother they couldn't do anything. Since Chelsea wouldn't implicate him, they couldn't even question him about statutory rape (having sex with a minor, a crime punishable in Kansas by at least 12 years in prison if convicted). So Mrs. Brooks tried to handle it herself—by calling Ray. "I don't want you around my daughter," she warned him. "Forget you ever knew her. I

*Name has been changed.

can't be responsible for what will happen to you if you continue to see her." Ray was totally calm. "She's just a friend," he said. "We talk on the phone sometimes." Mrs. Brooks didn't believe him, but there wasn't much else she could do.

Chelsea was desperate to *somehow* keep seeing Ray. On September 4, she wrote on her Xanga.com blog, "I love my boyfriend . . . and I want to be with him . . . but I just don't know what to do about all the people who don't want us to be together." She begged her friends to keep it a secret, and she often used their cell phones to call him.

TOUGH CHOICE

By that fall Chelsea was terrified—she realized she might be pregnant. In October she wrote on her blog, "I'm so stupid! I never should have done what I did and I wouldn't be in this situation." In December she asked her friend Kelsey Gresham to go with her to buy a test. Chelsea was devastated when the result was positive. "But she refused to believe it," Kelsey says. "She kept saying, 'It's wrong. It's wrong.'" She had taken five or six tests, and they were all positive. "There's no way you're not pregnant," Kelsey told her.

Chelsea didn't tell Ray—who she had been seeing off and on—until New Year's Eve, when she was three months pregnant. At first he seemed happy. But then he realized he could be charged with statutory rape. He was afraid the police would find out he was the father through DNA tests as soon as the baby was born. "I'll die if I'm put in jail," he told Chelsea. In early January 2006, Ray came up with a sick, violent plan to keep himself out of trouble. He suggested that they go to a school parking lot one night so he could kick her in the stomach to make her miscarry. Chelsea reluctantly agreed—until she told a friend, who talked her out of it.

The same month, one of Chelsea's classmates told her mom she'd heard Chelsea was pregnant. That mother notified an assistant principal, who alerted Mrs. Brooks. She confronted her daughter, and Chelsea admitted it was true. "I was trying not to explode I was so angry," Mrs. Brooks says. At first, still trying to protect Ray, Chelsea claimed the father was a 15-year-old friend, but she eventually admitted Ray was the real dad. Her parents discussed with her whether she should keep the baby or give it up for adoption. Then Mrs. Brooks asked Chelsea if she was still seeing Ray; her daughter said no. But since Chelsea had lied about him in the past, Mrs. Brooks didn't believe her. So on February 13, she went to the local courthouse and filed a petition for a protective order to *force* Ray to stay away from Chelsea. "The defendant has been in a sexual relationship with my minor daughter for at least 8 months," she wrote in the petition. "She is now pregnant, and he is psychologically manipulating her to keep secret the fact that he is the father." A judge ruled that Ray couldn't contact Chelsea or he would be arrested. Even so, months later Chelsea *still* had feelings for him. On June 5, she wrote on her blog, "I am sick to my stomach because of him!! I don't need him, so why do I dwell on what's never going to happen?? Get over it!!"

BRUTAL MURDER

On June 9, the night she was killed, Chelsea met some friends at 7 P.M. at Skate South, a popular skating rink and local hangout. Ray contacted her and asked her to meet him. Even though they hadn't been dating for months, she agreed, and Ray sent Everett to pick her up. Chelsea left the rink at 8 P.M. After Everett dropped off Chelsea at his sister's home and returned an hour later without Ray, Chelsea was furious. A little after 9 P.M., she sent a text message to her friends, who were waiting for her at the rink: "We're on our way back there. Ray stood me up. I'm mad." She also wrote that they had to drop off another guy on the way.

According to Everett's court testimony, minutes later Ted yanked the cord around Chelsea's neck and pulled it until she stopped kicking. Then the men drove to a secluded dirt road near a wheat field in Butler County, just outside Wichita. Ted dragged her body out of the car. He told Everett to bring a shovel and start digging a hole. Everett grabbed the shovel from the trunk and dug a shallow grave. Then Ted dropped Chelsea's body into the ground facedown and covered it with dirt.

When Chelsea didn't return to the rink, her friends got worried and called her parents, who then contacted the police. The next day they hung flyers all over town asking for help finding her. Then on June 14, two men working at the edge of the field where Chelsea had been buried found her body and called the police. The cops questioned Everett, the last person seen with her on the night she disappeared. He broke down and confessed that Ray had asked him to "get rid" of Chelsea and had offered Ted $500 to kill her. Police arrested Everett, Ray, and Ted, and they subsequently were charged with murder and other crimes. Everett has pleaded guilty and could be sentenced to life in prison; Ray and Ted could face the death penalty if they're found guilty.

Today Mr. Brooks grieves for his daughter. "Any guy that age who hits on a girl that young is a predator," he says. "By killing Chelsea, Ray thought he was gaining his freedom. But he may have lost it forever."

a mom
who loved
too much

**No one knows exactly what went down in
the schoolyard that day. But one thing is certain:
The neighborhood will never be the same.**

There was no limit to Miss Mary's love. She and her husband, a retired Amtrak mechanic named Larry Beard, raised 18 children of their own — 10 girls and eight boys, the youngest of whom is now 9. But even with all those kids, Miss Mary still had time for her many friends in her neighborhood in the Bronx, a part of New York City.

Miss Mary, at 50, was plump and smiling. She blew-dry her long, straight hair for special occasions; otherwise, she twisted it up into a bun. She sometimes wore a brown, fuzzy coat that her friends joked made her look like Fozzie Bear, and she carried a black pocketbook, straining at the seams, that could magically produce everything from meeting agendas and safety pins to Band-Aids and Tylenol. Miss Mary's smile was so beautiful that when she frowned, you would stand up straight, run to class, do whatever it was she told you to do — just so she would smile at you again.

Miss Mary and her family had lived in the Forest Houses projects for nearly 20 years, and everyone there knew her. If your mother needed a cake pan, Miss Mary would lend you one. Linda, 39, borrowed one pan so many times that Miss Mary said to Linda's daughter, "Tell your mother to keep it. If I need it, I'll borrow it from you." She was on the PTA at the middle school and the elementary school. Sometimes she cooked breakfast in the basement kitchen at the housing project where she lived and served it to the hungry.

But one thing about Miss Mary? She never minded her own business. Once, a man trying to break into a window of an apartment turned around and asked her just what, exactly she thought she was looking at. It turned out that the man lived there and had locked himself out.

Miss Mary said, "You should be glad I'm looking. What if someone was breaking into the house?"

The man backed down. "Yes ma'am," he said. "You're right. Thank you."

If Miss Mary was sitting on one of the park benches on Trinity Avenue, outside the apartment tower where the Beards lived on the fifth floor, parents knew they didn't have to worry about their children playing outside. Miss Mary would watch everyone's kids as if they were her own. If she saw a little kid out by himself, she would chase him on home. If she saw a fight, which happened often, she would break it up. No one would ever have guessed that it would be her Good Samaritan impulses that would lead to such tragedy.

A NORMAL DAY

The weather was finally nice in New York City, and Miss Mary was sitting on the park bench outside her building, waiting for her best friend, Gloria. They were going to the market, Western Beef, and then to the dollar store to get chocolate pudding and marshmallow pies for the kids. Across the street was the schoolyard of the elementary school, P.S. 146, where three of Miss Mary's young sons went, and on the next block down was I.S. 301, where her 13-year-old daughter, Yamilee, and Yamilee's friend Stinae were in sixth grade. The last bell rang just before 3:00, and Yamilee and Stinae started walking to the store to buy a pineapple soda.

Yamilee, whom everyone calls Yaya, is tall, slender, and tough, with hair that stands up like a lion's mane. She doesn't say much, except to note that she plays tackle football. She wants to be a lawyer, but she avoids the classes for smart kids. Stinae takes those. If you ask Yaya what she wants to tell the world about herself, she says, "Don't come near me."

Stinae has intricate braids that creep along her skull, weaving under and over each other. She is skinny, but it's easy to see that she's tough too. Stinae had a simmering feud with an older high school girl, who claimed that Stinae's brother was trying to beat up her brother. The high school girl threatened to hit Stinae's brother, which upset Stinae because the high school girl was so much bigger than either of them.

WHO STARTED IT?

That fateful day, when Yaya, Stinae, and their friends reached the tree-shaded corner of the block where the elementary school sits, the older girl appeared. She said something to Stinae that Stinae, when she was telling the story later, did not want to repeat because it was too rude. Yaya says Stinae hit the high school girl in the face and she deserved it. Stinae says she didn't hit the older girl. But either way, everyone started drifting toward the P.S. 146 schoolyard. One of the

119

neighborhood boys egged them on. "She wants to fight y'all; she wants to fight y'all!" he taunted Stinae.

The schoolyard is pure inner city: a sea of asphalt in front of a squat, ugly school with burglar bars. It is dotted with basketball hoops and surrounded by a tall chain-link fence, and the only color comes from a series of murals painted by Yaya's class when she was in fifth grade, the year the World Trade Center fell. On the biggest segment of wall, set apart from all the rest, is Yaya's mural of the New York City skyline at sunset, with red and white billowing stripes on either side.

It was in front of this wall that the fight broke out. "We started throwing our hands, and I took a swing at her," says Stinae. Soon the fight became a brawl, involving at least 10 people Yaya can list by name— cousins, siblings, friends of both Stinae and the older girl—and a bunch of people she didn't know.

Yaya says she did not get into it until Stinae was knocked to the ground. "I felt like if I didn't jump in, my friend wasn't going to trust me anymore," says Yaya. "And she's my best friend." Yaya went right for the older girl, swinging her fists. All around her, people were fighting. Quanta, Stinae's littlest brother, was getting kicked. One of Stinae's friends picked Stinae up with one hand and pounded a girl with the other.

MARY GETS INVOLVED

It was then that the crowd of onlookers parted to make way for Miss Mary. She was not running, but she was walking fast, straight into the melee, where she grabbed Yaya by the hood of her gray sweatshirt. Some people say that when Miss Mary tried to stop the fight, a boy kicked her. Others say she dropped to her knees. And some people said they saw a girl jump on her back

120

and punch her from behind. "I think the girl was trying to get at me," Yaya says.

It was not long—maybe a minute—before Miss Mary emerged from the circle of people. She was breathing hard, and she went over to the chain-link fence and held on to it, slumped over, her chest heaving up and down. Gradually people started to notice that Miss Mary was not okay. The circle opened, and the fight stopped. Yaya had never seen her mother have a bad asthma attack before—her mother who put chicken or ribs on the table every night, who got antsy if she had two minutes to relax, who charged down the halls at school with her bulging pocketbook.

So at that moment, Yaya didn't realize the seriousness of her mom's condition. She was more worried about Stinae, who'd gotten knocked around in the fight, and began to walk her friend home. Meanwhile, the schoolyard filled with teachers, security guards, and people from Miss Mary's buildings. The older girls who had been fighting fled. Gloria came running up to the fence. "I can't breathe," Miss Mary told her, and then she collapsed. "I can't breathe," she said again to Larry, her husband, who was down on the asphalt at her side.

Stinae, meanwhile, turned out to be just bruised, and Yaya headed back toward her own house. At the schoolyard, she saw a large circle of people and an ambulance with flashing lights. Yaya stopped. She did not want to get any closer. "I was too scared," she says. When she is asked what she thought was happening, she just shakes her head and looks at the ground.

Yaya went up to her apartment, where one of her older sisters told her what had happened: Their mother

121

was dead. The medical examiner reported that Miss Mary died of an asthma attack following intervention in an altercation, which means that if she hadn't tried to break up the fight, she probably would not have died.

THE NEIGHBORHOOD MOURNS

Miss Mary was a Jehovah's Witness, but her church was not nearly big enough to accommodate all the people who came to her funeral. To begin with, there were the children and the grandchildren. Then there were the people from the neighborhood. Then there were the VIPs, like the school district superintendent and a representative from the borough president's office. Miss Mary was well loved in her own right, but the way she died made her an outright hero.

"I think the kids knew their mother was important," a family friend says. "But I don't think they realized how important until they saw how many people loved her."

Life is different now in the Beard home. Yaya's father, a quiet, understanding man with a peaceful air, cooks the dinners. Sometimes he wears a T-shirt with a photo of Miss Mary on the front, and a photo on the back of Belinda, his daughter who died when she was 23, also of an asthma attack. MAMA OF THE BIG OL' FAMILY, the front says. DADDY'S LITTLE GIRL, the back says. Now that he takes care of both the children and the grandchildren, Larry has his own nickname: Grandpa Mama.

Larry seems almost not to realize that there has been a lot of talk around the neighborhood about who was responsible for Miss Mary's death. Some people say it was the school security guards, who witnesses say were nowhere to be found when the fight started. Some say it was the fault of the older girls, who have never been seen in the neighborhood again.

122

But hardest of all for Yaya and Stinae is the idea that they might be to blame. Yaya's older sister tells Yaya that it was not her fault. "But," Yaya says, staring down at the blacktop where it happened, and where, two months later, her brother and Stinae's brothers are now playing basketball, "I still say it is."

Daquan, an 11-year-old who is also playing basketball, complains that he doesn't like it that now, every time there is a problem, his principal brings up Miss Mary's name to remind the students of the dire consequences of fighting. On the other hand, he says, what happened to Miss Mary "should teach people a lesson."

"It taught *some* people a lesson," Yaya says, meaning herself. "I learned that if it's a fight between your friends, you got to walk away from it; but if it's family, you can get involved. My mother told us we have to stick by each other. She told us not to betray each other for nobody."

contributors

index